CAMBRIDGE LIBRARY COLLECTION

Books of enduring scholarly value

British and Irish History, Seventeenth and Eighteenth Centuries

The books in this series focus on the British Isles in the early modern period, as interpreted by eighteenth- and nineteenth-century historians, and show the shift to 'scientific' historiography. Several of them are devoted exclusively to the history of Ireland, while others cover topics including economic history, foreign and colonial policy, agriculture and the industrial revolution. There are also works in political thought and social theory, which address subjects such as human rights, the role of women, and criminal justice.

An Essay upon Money and Coins

Joseph Harris (1704–64) was equally distinguished as an astronomer and as an expert on coinage. From a humble background, he came to the attention of Edmond Halley, the Astronomer Royal. He spent some time making astronomical observations in South America and the West Indies, and familiarised himself with marine navigational practice, proposing improvements to measuring equipment and publishing a very popular instructional work on the uses of globes and orreries. He later observed the 1761 transit of Venus from Wales. Harris entered the Royal Mint in 1736, and became the King's Assay Master in 1749. This influential 1757 work, considered by the Victorian economist J.R. McCulloch as 'one of the best and most valuable treatises on the subject of money that has ever seen the light', argues that it is vital to a country's economy that the value of precious metal in its coinage remains constant.

Cambridge University Press has long been a pioneer in the reissuing of out-of-print titles from its own backlist, producing digital reprints of books that are still sought after by scholars and students but could not be reprinted economically using traditional technology. The Cambridge Library Collection extends this activity to a wider range of books which are still of importance to researchers and professionals, either for the source material they contain, or as landmarks in the history of their academic discipline.

Drawing from the world-renowned collections in the Cambridge University Library and other partner libraries, and guided by the advice of experts in each subject area, Cambridge University Press is using state-of-the-art scanning machines in its own Printing House to capture the content of each book selected for inclusion. The files are processed to give a consistently clear, crisp image, and the books finished to the high quality standard for which the Press is recognised around the world. The latest print-on-demand technology ensures that the books will remain available indefinitely, and that orders for single or multiple copies can quickly be supplied.

The Cambridge Library Collection brings back to life books of enduring scholarly value (including out-of-copyright works originally issued by other publishers) across a wide range of disciplines in the humanities and social sciences and in science and technology.

An Essay upon Money and Coins

JOSEPH HARRIS

CAMBRIDGE
UNIVERSITY PRESS

CAMBRIDGE
UNIVERSITY PRESS

University Printing House, Cambridge, CB2 8BS, United Kingdom

Cambridge University Press is part of the University of Cambridge.
It furthers the University's mission by disseminating knowledge in the pursuit of
education, learning and research at the highest international levels of excellence.

www.cambridge.org
Information on this title: www.cambridge.org/9781108078573

© in this compilation Cambridge University Press 2017

This edition first published 1757
This digitally printed version 2017

ISBN 978-1-108-07857-3 Paperback

AN ESSAY UPON MONEY and COINS.

PART I.

The Theories of COMMERCE, MONEY, and EXCHANGES.

LONDON,

Printed: Sold by G. HAWKINS at the *Middle Temple Gate, Fleet-ſtreet*. M.DCC.LVII.

To the Honourable

RICHARD ARUNDELL, *Efq*;

As a teftimony of Efteem for his great
Worth and Abilities, and as a grateful
acknowlegement for many Marks of his
Favour and Regard, during a long courfe
of years; this Tract

Is humbly Infcribed and Dedicated, by

His moft faithful

and obedient Servant,

THE AUTHOR.

PREFACE.

THE main part of the following essay, was drawn up many years since for a truly great and good man; one who, if it had pleased God to have continued his life but a little longer, intended, amidst his other great designs for the good of this country, to have made such regulations in regard to our coins, as probably would have obviated all complaints about them for the future. The chief design of this first part, is to unfold the true nature and theory of money: A subject wherein every one is interested, and that in some measure in proportion to his property; and yet, a subject it seems, that very few understand; and concerning which, many, and those too of some note, are under gross mistakes.

In order to clear the way, and for the better settling of things upon their first and true principles, it hath been thought necessary to take a general view of wealth and commerce, which is the subject of the first chapter; and the third, concerning exchanges, is not quite foreign to the main design.

Some of the points here touched upon, deserved to have been discussed more. at large, if the designed brevity of the whole would have permitted. The author is clear as to the goodness of his intention, and hopes that his ill state of health, while these sheets were printing, will be admitted as an apology for such faults as may have happened in the execution.

THE

[vi]

THE

CONTENTS.

CHAP.

CHAP. II. Of MONEY and COINS.

Any

Chap. III. Of exchanges.

PART

PART I.

The Theories of COMMERCE, MONEY, *and* EXCHANGES.

CHAPTER I.

Of the nature and origin of wealth and commerce.

I. *Of wealth, what, and wherein it confifts.*

1. THE earth abounds with an infinite variety of materials, for the comfortable fubfiftence of human life : Befides the great diverfity of food, vegetable and animal, more than fufficient to fatiate the moft gluttonous appetite ; how admirably are wood, ftones, metals, &c. adapted to their various ufes ! What is there left unprovided, and of what kind is that other material that could have added to human conveniency ? But amidft this vaft profufion of things, the earth fpontaneoufly produces but few that are ready fitted for our ufe : Some pains and induftry are required on our part, without which,

Land and labour, the fources of all wealth

B   our

our condition upon this globe would, perhaps, be the moſt forlorn and uncomfortable of any of its inhabitants. But of this we have no cauſe to complain : Labour or bodily exerciſe, in a certain degree, is not only eaſy but pleaſant to us, conducive to our health, and every way ſuited to our nature; and we are endued with ample powers for adopting and fitting the materials about us, according to our various exigencies and occaſions. Land and labour together are the ſources of all wealth; without a competency of land, there would be no ſubſiſtence; and but a very poor and uncomfortable one, without labour. So that *wealth* or *riches* conſiſt either in a propriety in land, or in the products of land and labour.

In wealthy countries, the value of the labour is much greater than that of the land.

2. The proportional values of land and product, differ very much in different countries; as the ſoils are reſpectively more or leſs fertil, and the inhabitants more or leſs induſtrious, and ſkilful. Without ſome kind of tillage, much land will be requiſite to maintain a few inhabitants ; and a ſmall field of wheat will afford nouriſhment to more people, than a large foreſt yielding nothing but
acorns

acorns and wild fruits. The annual produce of labour in *England*, I imagine, is of
much greater value than the rent of the
land; but their exact proportion to each
other, cannot be eafily affigned. It is commonly fuppofed that a farmer, to be enabled to live comfortably, muft make three
rents of his land; and when we confider
the coarfenefs of thofe commodities, that are
commonly expended in a farmer's houfe, in
comparifon of many others confumed by
thofe of more affluent fortunes; the value
of labour to that of land, muft be with us
greater than that of 2 to 1. Wool wrought
into cloth is much advanced in its value;
thread may be of above 100 times the value of the flax whereof it was made. The
value of the materials in * watches, and
innumerable other things made of metals,
is but fmall in comparifon of the value of
the workmanfhip. But we muft not purfue this notion too far : The numbers employed about thefe coftly things, may not
bear a large proportion to thofe who are
either idle, or occupied about tillage, buildings, or other manufacturies; where the raw
materials are worth near as much, or fometimes more, than the labour beftowed upon
B 2 them.

* The balance fpring in a good watch is worth above a
million of times the value of the fteel.

them.   The *Britiſh merchant* computes the
value of labour to that of land in *England*
to be as 7 to 2 *.   He ſuppoſes the people
of *England* to be 7 millions, and each man
at a medium to expend 7 pounds each, which
makes the whole annual conſumption of
England 49 millions ; 45 millions of which
he ſuppoſes to be our own product, 4 millions

* This ſhews the great value of arts and induſtry.   But
their uſefulneſs doth not terminate in the mere value of their
productions ; their benign influence extends much farther.
By furniſhing employment, at the ſame time, both to the mind
and body ; they tend to improve the underſtanding, to hu-
maniſe mankind, and to preſerve them from that brutal bar-
bariſm, which is ever the attendant of ſtupid indolence and
inactivity.   Each individual, by a laudable induſtry, ſtriving
to benefit himſelf ; the whole community ſhare the fruits,
and peace and good order is every where maintained.
But here occurs a difficult queſtion ; how to employ uſe-
fully all that are fit and able to work, and to maintain comfortably ſuch as cannot help themſelves ?   Our indulgent
parent hath ſo ordered things, that it ſhould not be neceſſary
for all to work : Some compute, that the labour of one-fourth
of the people is ſufficient to maintain the other three-fourths ;
that one-fourth, as infants, old people, &c. are quite help-
leſs ; that one-fourth live upon their lands ; whence one-
fourth are left for the learned profeſſions, ſtate offices, and for
being merchants, ſhopkeepers, ſoldiers, &c.   Here then are
three parts that are mere conſumers ; and as a country grows
in wealth, the candidates for genteel employments may become more numerous in proportion to the reſt, perhaps too
much ſo for the land and labour to maintain : And thus, too
many expecting a livelihood without labour ; murmurs, complaints of the decay of trade, want of money, &c. will be
loud.   Amongſt the lower claſs, ſome profeſſions at times
will be naturally overſtocked : But if there be want of employments upon the whole, there muſt be ſome defect in
our police ; as the produce of *England* is undoubtedly ſufficient, to employ and maintain comfortably, a much greater
number of inhabitants.

lions foreign commodities; and the rents
of the lands he makes 14 millions.

II. *Values of things, how estimated.*

3. Things in general are valued, not according to their real uses in supplying the
necessities of men ; but rather in proportion
to the land, labour and skill that are requi-
site to produce them : It is according to
this proportion nearly, that things or commodities are exchanged one for another;
and it is by the said scale, that the intrinsic
values of most things are chiefly estimated.
Water is of great use, and yet ordinarily of
little or no value; because in most places, water flows spontaneously in such great plenty,
as not to be with-held within the limits of
private property; but all may have enough,
without other expence than that of bringing or conducting it, when the case so requires.   On the other hand, diamonds, being
very scarce, have upon that account a great
value, though they are but of little use.   A
quicker or flower demand for a particular
commodity, will frequently raise or lower
its price, though no alteration hath happened in its intrinsic value or prime cost ; men
being always ready to take the advantage of

one another's fancies, whims or neceffities; and the proportion of buyers to fellers, or the demand for any particular commodity in refpect to its quantity, will always have an influence on the market. The intrinfic value of a particular commodity may be alfo enhanced, though its quality is debafed ; as a bufhel of mufty grain at one feafon, may be worth much more, than the like quantity of good grain at another.

Cheapnefs, how eftimated.

4. Commodities are called bulky or faid to be * cheap, which bear but a fmall proportion of value to others of equal bulk ; and thefe are natural products, either growing fpontaneoufly, or requiring no great art and labour in their cultivation ; as grain of all forts, cattle for food or labour, timber and ftone for building, fuel, &c. The goodnefs of Providence having fo ordered things, that thofe main fupports of life fhould abound every where, according to the exigencies of different climates. And of metals, that moft ufeful one, iron, is in our happy clime the cheapeft.

Natural

---

* Things are alfo faid to be cheap or dear, in refpect to the prices they bore at fome former market.

Natural produ&s, &c. *fubje& to a greater variation in their value, than artificial.*

5. The quantity of corn, &c. produced from the fame number of acres, and from the fame quantity of labour, being fometimes very different, according to the difference of feafons; grain of all forts, as alfo cattle from mortality amongft them, or other cafualties, are fubje& to much greater variations in their values, than artificial produ&s; and a bufhel of corn may be worth twice or thrice as much cloth, at one time as at another. Corn muft be had; and the farmers will endeavour to make as much of their fmall ftock, as when they had a greater plenty; on the other hand, when the market is full, they muft lower their price; till, after reckoning the value of the land, the labour beftowed in raifing a bufhel of corn, and in fabricating the thing for which it is exchanged, are on both fides nearly equal. Things of a more limited vent, are fubje& to vary yet more from their ufual price, than corn; as apples, hops, &c.

Things

*Things are the more valued, the farther they
    are from the place where they were firſt
    produced.*

6. Things near the place where they are
produced, whether by nature or art, have
naturally a leſs value in proportion to other
things, than they have in places more remote ; and this in proportion to the riſques
of all ſorts, and expences of carriage.   Silver is naturally cheaper in *Mexico* than in
Spain, and in *Spain* than in the reſt of
Europe.   Things that are rare, or for which
there is no great demand, are generally
dearer than in the above proportion : For,
when there are but few dealers in any commodity, they ſeldom fail to enhance its price,
and that ſometimes very exorbitantly.   One
great myſtery of trade, is to keep off new
adventurers, by concealing its profits ; and
whilſt that may be done, the gains will be
large.

III. *The price of labour, the chief ſtandard
     that regulates the values of all things.*

7. The values of land and labour do, as
it were of themſelves, mutually ſettle or ad-
juſt one another ; and as all things or commodities, are the products of thoſe two ; ſo
                                        their

their feveral values are naturally adjufted by them. But as in moft productions, *labour* hath the greateft fhare ; the value of labour is to be reckoned the chief ftandard that regulates the values of all commodities ; and more efpecially as the value of land is, as it were, already allowed for in the value of labour itfelf.

Men's various neceffities and appetites, oblige them to part with their own com-modities, at a rate proportionable to the labour and fkill that had been beftowed upon thofe things, which they want in ex-change : If they will not comply with the market, their goods will remain on their hands ; and if at firft, one trade be more pro-fitable than another, fkill as well as labour and rifques of all forts, being taken into the account ; more men will enter into that bufinefs, and in their outvying will under-fell one another, till at length the great pro-fit of it is brought down to a *par* with the reft.

Some eftimate of the value of labour.

8. It may be reafonably allowed, that a labouring man ought to earn at leaft, twice as much as will maintain himfelf in ordi-nary food and cloathing ; that he may be

enabled

enabled to breed up children, pay rent
for a fmall dwelling, find himfelf in neceffary utenfils, &c. So much at leaft the
labourer muft be allowed, that the community may be perpetuated : And as the
world goes, there is no likelihood that the
loweft kind of labourers will be allowed
more than a bare fubfiftence ; if they will
not be content with that, there will be others
ready to ftep into their places; and lefs, as
above obferved, cannot be given them. And
hence the quantity of * land that goes to
maintain a labourer, becomes his hire; and
this hire again becomes the value of the land;
the expences of manuring and tilling it, being
alfo included. There is a difference in the
proportion of the value of an acre of land to a
given quantity of labour, all over the world;
and this arifeth, not only from the different
goodnefs of the land, but alfo from the different ways of living of the peafants in different places. For, where labour is very
cheap, that is, where the labourers live very
poorly, land will be alfo cheap ; as the
poor, from their numbers, are the principal
confumers of the groffer products of the
earth.

* Lands yielding uncommon products, as mines, &c.
are not here confidered ; the uncommonnefs of them gives
an opportunity to the owners of making more than ordinary
profit by fuch products.

earth. So that every where, I think, the price of land is influenced by the price of labour ; that is, by the quality of food and raiment confumed by the labourers; for of fome fort, they muft have a fufficient quantity : It feems then to be no good policy in the rich to deal too hardly with the poor; befides, that fuch treatment muft needs greatly check arts and induftry, difcourage matrimony amongft the lower clafs, and infpire them with thoughts of quitting their homes, in hopes of bettering their ftate elfewhere.   But the benevolence here hinted at, is to be tempered with difcretion : The children of the poor fhould be brought up and inured, as early as may be, to fome ufeful labour; and be taught with due care, the great principles of religion and morality.   But all are not agreed that reading and writing, are qualifications neceffary for the obtaining of thofe ends ; fome think, that thefe accomplifhments are ufeful only in higher ftations ; and that to inftruct at a public expence the youth of the lower clafs in reading, writing, &c. is a kind of intrufion upon the clafs next above them ; that thefe qualifications, inftead of being advantageous to the poor who poffefs them, ferve only to render their ftate more irkfome, and to infpire them

with

with notions fubverfive of fociety. There
muft be labourers; and that moft ufeful clafs
of men fhould be duly cherifhed and taken
care of: But books and pens will not alle-
viate the weight of the fpade, or at all contribute to dry the fweat off the labourer's
brow.

Charitable contributions necefary.

9. The price of labour being fixed, fo
that one labourer can earn about twice as
much, or fomething more, than what will
maintain himfelf; if he has feveral young
children, a fickly wife, an aged and helplefs parent, or is himfelf difabled; he will
want, and will have a right to afk, the charitable aid of fome of his opulent neighbours :
It is therefore almoft unavoidable, but that
fome of the loweft clafs will be deftitute of
fubfiftence, who muft or ought to be maintained and taken due care of, by public
contributions or eftablifhments *. If a man
be fingle, he will earn as much as the married man; for no regard to a man's circumftances will be had in the price of his labour; and fo the fingle man may feed and
clothe himfelf better than the other; and
if

---

* Great care fhould be taken that all charitable contributions are duly applied to their proper objects, and are not
embezzled or wantonly fquandered.

if he is frugal, he will fave fomewhat
againft he is married, which little favings
may enable him to live more comfortably
all the reft of his life.

Mechanics earn more than labourers, &c.

10. To bring up a child to a trade, there
is not only an expence in fitting him out,
and during his apprenticefhip, but alfo a
rifque of his dying before he is out of his
time; from which confiderations a mechanic
is entitled to better wages than a common
labourer : And as any given trade is attended with greater rifques of any fort, requires
more fkill, more truft, more expence in fetting up, &c. the artificer will be entitled
to ftill better wages. In like manner, thofe
profeffions that require genius, great confi-
dence, a liberal education, &c. have a right
to be rewarded proportionably. And thus,
the prices of labour and fervices of different forts, have a confiderable difference
founded in the nature of them : But the
wages of the lower clafs, wherein is to be
included, as well the common artificers
as the hufbandmen, feems to be the main
and ultimate ftandard that regulates the
values of all commodities; and if thofe
wages be regulated by and paid in bullion,
that

2

that fpecific bullion will be the true and real
money of the country where it is fo applied, notwithftanding what elfe may pafs in
greater tranfactions.

IV. *Of trade or commerce.*

11. By the wife appointment of divine
Providence, a mutual intercourfe and commerce amongft men, is both conducive and
neceffary to their well being.   Every man
ftands in need of the aid of others; and
every country may reap advantages, by exchanging fome of its fuperfluous products,
natural or artificial, for thofe which it wants
of foreign growth.

The firft employments that a colony of
people, newly fettled in an uncultivated
country, would naturally fall upon, would
be to clear, till and fow, or plant the ground
with feeds and roots proper for their nou-
rifhment; and to provide themfelves with
fome kind of dwellings and garments, to
fhelter and protect them from the incle-
mencies of the weather : In order to obtain
which, they would foon find themfelves
under the neceffity, and feel the comforts,
of affociating together, and of eftablifhing a
certain mode or form of government.   For,
all the labour and fkill of any one man, or

of

of any one family unconnected with others, would fcarce be able to procure them the common neceffaries of food and cloathing; and much lefs would they be ever able to furnifh themfelves with thofe various conveniencies, which we now fo plentifully enjoy.

Men are endued with various talents and propenfities, which naturally difpofe and fit them for different occupations; and are, as above obferved, under a neceffity of betaking themfelves to particular arts and employments, from their inability of otherwife acquiring all the neceffaries they want, with eafe and comfort *: This creates a dependance of one man upon another, and naturally unites men into focieties. In like manner, as all countries differ more or lefs, either in the kinds or goodnefs of their products, natural or artificial; particular men find their advantages, which extend to communities in general, by trading with the remoteft nations.

It was the neceffities of men that gave birth to the arts, and long experience hath brought many of them to a furprizing degree

* The mutual conveniencies accruing to individuals, from their betaking themfelves to particular occupations, is perhaps the chief cement that connects them together; the main fource of commerce, and of large political communities.

gree of perfection. The moſt curious arts
now ſubſiſting are the growth of *Europe*,
and chiefly of the laſt and preſent age;
and herein, our own country hath much to
boaſt of *.

Uſefulneſs of diſtinct trades, farther illuſtrated.

12. The advantages accruing to mankind
from their betaking themſelves ſeverally to
different occupations, are very great and
obvious:

* The name of NEWTON, to omit many others of great
eminence in different kinds of knowledge, will do honour
to this nation, whilſt men continue civilized, and preſerve
the ſciences amongſt them. We have lately loſt a mechanic, whoſe aſſiſtance on many occaſions was eagerly courted,
even by our vain and rival neighbours; a man well known,
and, being known, admired, in all the principal courts,
and learned academies of *Europe*. I need not ſay that I here
mean the late GEORGE GRAHAM, whoſe eminent ſkill in
mechanics, by which he was known to the world, was yet
known to his friends to have been but a ſmall part of his
merit. We have yet ſeveral artiſts who excel in their reſpective profeſſions, all that went before them. What
Mr. HARRISON hath done about *clocks*, is truly admirable;
and *mathematical inſtruments* were never made ſo perfect and
exact, as they have been and ſtill are by Mr. BIRD: Theſe
men ſtand unrivalled. I have many more very excellent
artiſts in my eye, but I forbear naming any, leſt I ſhould do
injuſtice to others who might have an equal ſhare of merit.
Whilſt I am celebrating the ſuperior ſkill of ſome of our
moſt eminent artiſts, I am not very wide from my ſubject:
And I wiſh it was duly conſidered, by thoſe who ought to
conſider it, what countenance and encouragement is due to
ſuch men; what great benefactors they are to their country,
what great reputation and wealth they bring to it, who by
their fame and example create emulation in others, and ſo
raiſe and ſupport a reputation of our artificial products in
diſtant countries.

obvious: For thereby, each becoming expert and skilful in his own particular art; they are enabled to furnish one another with the products of their respective labours, performed in a much better manner, and with much less toil, than any one of them could do of himself *. And the world now abounds with vastly greater quantities and varieties of artificial products, than could ever have been effected by the utmost efforts of small and unconnected societies. The farmer is the most likely person to be able to subsist of himself; but he would find it very difficult to get even implements for his husbandry, without the aid of the smith and the carpenter; and they again, find it their interest to truck with him for what they want, instead of tilling the ground themselves. In building and furnishing a house, the business

---

* When our great load of taxes, reaching down to the meanest artificer, is considered; it would seem that labour is cheaper in *England* than in other countries; that is, that our artificers are more skilful, and produce more and better goods in a given time, than is usually done elsewhere: For, in comparing the price of labour, the mere consumptions or earnings of the labourers, are not alone sufficient; what their labour produces, must be also taken into the account. Without supposing that labour, in effect, is really cheap with us, it would be difficult to account how such large quantities of our artificial products could be vended abroad. But how long this supposed superiority of our workmen, can be able to balance our other disadvantages, deserves seriously to be considered.

C

finefs becomes ftill more complex; and more variety of arts are neceffary. And fhould any one undertake to provide a coat only, by going himfelf through the various operations of fhearing the wool, carding, fpinning, weaving, tucking, &c. half the labour and toil in his own particular profeffion, would not only have equipped him with a better garment, but alfo procured him other neceffaries *. Befides the great incumbrance of tools, that would be requifite for the finifhing of moft things from the beginning; it would be next to impoffible for any one man, either to find time, or to acquire fkill fufficient, for the making of all thofe tools; he would foon find himfelf at a lofs, and under a neceffity of feeking the aid of others.

Ufefulnefs of dealers.

13. The ufefulnefs of people betaking and confining themfelves to particular arts, is very manifeft. And from hence naturally arife employments for another clafs of men; I mean, dealers of all forts, from the meaneft fhop-keeper to the merchant: Thefe, without

* Agreeable to this is the old *adage*, " Jack-of-all-trades " will never be rich." And thofe fmattering geniufes who will be meddling in various arts, rather than employ others in their proper callings, are but poor œconomifts, as well as bad neighbours.

out applying themfelves to any of the manual arts, are bufied in collecting, and afterwards in diftributing, the various forts of products or commodities; and by their arts and induftry, the products of the remoteft places are collected, as it were, into grand ftore-houfes; where every one may be readily fupplied, according to his defires.

The dealers, like the artificers, are fubdivided into diftinct trades, and fo, become mutually ferviceable to each other. Without this fubdivifion, commerce would have been ftrangely embarraffed; many parts of it muft have been totally neglected; and a monopoly here would have like bad effects, as if men tried themfelves to make all the things they wanted.

Ufefulnefs of commerce farther exemplified.

14. To exemplify the nature of commerce a little more particularly: Amidft the farmers, which we will fuppofe are difperfed at convenient diftances over the whole country, there will be villages of different fizes, difperfed at yet greater diftances. In thefe villages, befides fome farmers, and fome poor hufbandmen; there will be moft likely a fmith, a carpenter, an alehoufe-keeper, perhaps a butcher; if not

a ſhoe-maker, at leaſt a cobler, a petty gro-
cer, &c.   In larger villages, there will be
more of theſe trades, and ſome others beſides : All theſe have their food of the
neighbouring farmers, and are ſupported by
what they earn of them, and of one another.   Their overplus, the farmers carry
to the adjacent market-towns ; wherein are a
greater number, and a greater variety of artificers; more ſhops, and better ſorts of goods;
more publicans, and better entertainments,
than are in the villages.   The ſeveral ſhop-
keepers here, fetching many or moſt of
their goods from remote places, in large
quantities at a time, can afford to furniſh
their reſpective cuſtomers at a much cheaper
rate, than they could furniſh themſelves ; as
they ſave each of them the trouble, riſque,
loſs of time, and expence of a long journey.
Theſe ſhop-keepers know alſo, how to procure their goods at the beſt hand; and they
take care to furniſh themſelves, with whatever is neceſſary for the conſumption of
the adjacent country.   The farmers, like-
wiſe, find it their advantage to diſpoſe of
their ſuperfluous cattle, butter, cheeſe, &c.
to drovers and chapmen, that come to meet
them at known appointed fairs ; and they
again, know where to drive and carry, by
                                            whole-

wholefale, thofe commodities to a better market,

The trade of large towns, is again branched out into greater varieties; thefe not only fupplying the leffer towns, as they do the villages, but alfo affording many curiofities, fit only for the gentry and people of affluent fortunes. In like manner, manufacturers and dealers, find it their intereft to feek each other: Knowing before-hand where and how to difpofe of his goods; the one, is enabled to purfue and cultivate his art, without that lofs of time and interruption, to which he would be otherwife liable; and the other, having in his warehoufe various fortments of different goods, bought at the beft hand from different manufacturers, furnifhes not only the petty fhop-keepers or chapmen of his neighbourhood, but alfo many others in remote places, with all the forts they want; which would have been endlefs and too expenfive for them to have done, by going themfelves for their little quantities to the feveral manufacturies, which might be difperfed at great diftances.

Thus, as in the manual arts, it is the intereft of each dealer, to confine himfelf within a certain diftrict; and this, likewife, is of mutual advantage to the whole: By this œconomy, each particular trade becomes better

under-

...lerſtood, better cultivated, and carried on
...fier and cheaper; the whole community
..., as it were, thereby linked together in one
general commerce; and by a daily intercourſe
and correſpondence, a large country becomes
in effect as one great city ; greater numbers,
creating more employments, and contributing
to each other's better ſubſiſtence : It being
a conſtant obſervation, that the pooreſt living is in thin inhabited countries. Indeed,
it is trade that makes countries populous,
as well as what procures the inhabitants a
comfortable ſubſiſtence. Again, by the diligence of the merchant, in inveſtigating and
diſperſing the products of different countries; all nations become, as it were, connected together in a commercial intereſt ;
and all enjoy the benefits of the various productions of different climates.

Of foreign commerce.

15. In a nation ſkilful in arts, and abounding in products for the neceſſaries of life;
the due ordering of its own internal trade,
muſt be its greateſt concern : But yet foreign commerce is advantageous, in many
reſpects. By the great and almoſt inexpli-
cable circuit and labyrinth of trade, the peculiar riches of each reſpective country, are
                                    diſperſed

difperfed every where, to the mutual benefit of all mankind; and the whole world becomes, as it were, one community or great trading city; every climate, by the means of commerce, enjoying the peculiar fruits of the reft: By commerce, not only commodities natural and artificial, but the arts themfelves are alfo communicated, improved, and extended; induftry promoted, and ufeful employments found for a greater number of hands. There is perhaps no nation in the world, but what might fubfift of itfelf; moft countries abounding with means of fuftaining life, fuitable to their refpective climates; and yet, perhaps, there is no country fo fertil, or nation fo polite, but what may be greatly benefited by a foreign commerce. In the *Weft-Indies*, where labour is toilfome, a fmall degree of it fuffices to procure plenty of roots for bread; and a fufficiency of flefh, fifh, and fowl, are eafily obtained. But the artificial products of *Europe*, are a beneficial exchange for the produce of the cane; and this again is convenient and acceptable to the *Europeans*.

Every nation fhould have a watchful eye over its foreign commerce; for it might fo happen, that a trade which enriches the merchant, might impoverifh the public.

That

That trade is moſt beneficial, which exports thoſe commodities that are leaſt wanted at home, and upon which moſt labour
hath been beſtowed ; and which brings in
return the reverſe ſort ; that is, ſimple pro-
duds, either neceſſary for immediate conſumption, in the form they are imported ;
or as materials to be wrought into commodities, wanted either for home uſe
or exportation. In few words, that trade
is beſt, which tends moſt to promote induſtry at home, by finding employment
for moſt hands ; and which furniſhes the
nation with ſuch foreign commodities, as
are either uſeful and neceſſary for our defence, or more comfortable ſubſiſtence. And
that trade is the worſt, that exports the
leaſt of the produd of labour ; that furniſhes
materials for manufaduries in other countries, which afterwards might interfere with
ſome of its own ; and which brings home
unneceſſary commodities, either ſoon pe-
riſhable, or of a precarious value. But no
nation can in all caſes chuſe for itſelf : The
immediate diſadvantages of ſome trades are
to be overlooked, if in the long run and
great circle of commerce, they at laſt turn
out to be beneficial. Natural alliances, and
                                        natural

natural rivalſhips, for ſuch there are, and
ever will be, betwixt particular nations, are
alſo ſubjects of great moment to the ſtateſman, though not to the merchant, in the
conſideration of a beneficial commerce. And
to a maritime country, the increaſe of ſhip-
ping and of mariners, is an object of great
importance.

I am unwarily entered upon a large field;
but my view under this head, being only
to give a general idea of the nature and benefit of trade, by ſketching out ſome of the
principal lines, I muſt here proceed no farther: To treat this ſubject with tolerable
accuracy, would be a large, curious and uſeful undertaking *.

V.

* This would be no leſs, than the taking a general view
of the whole political œconomy of eſtabliſhed communities;
it would be ſhewing how the ſeveral parts are neceſſarily connected, mutually dependent on and ſubſervient to each other,
and to the whole : Such a work might be of ſingular uſe to
the ſtateſman, by pointing out to him, what parts are growing too luxuriant, and what parts want further nouriſhment
and countenance; and perhaps, in the whole ſyſtem of po-
litics, if the whole doth not ultimately terminate there,
no part is of that importance as the preſerving of a due
order in all things at home.

How trades beget and nouriſh each other, is beautifully
deſcribed in a book, containing many judicious obſervations upon that ſubject, entitled, *A plan of the Engliſh commerce*, page 20 to 27. The author, after ſuppoſing fifty
farmers, each with two hundred pounds ſtock, ſettled in a
kind of circle of a convenient extent in ſome uninhabited
part of *England*, ſhews how in a little time a town with various trades, would be naturally built and ſettled in the
midſt

V. *Of the comparative riches or wealth of nations.*

16. The comparative riches and ftrength of nations, are not to be reckoned from the extent of their dominions, or fimply from their numbers of people; but rather from the fertility and aptnefs of the foil, for furnifhing ufeful and neceffary products; from the induftry of the inhabitants, and their fkilfulnefs in arts; and befides all this, from their having a well-modelled, and well-adminiftered government: For a good government is itfelf a moft valuable treafure, a main fource of riches, and of all temporal bleffings. The *Ruffian* map, takes in a larger extent of country than all *Europe*; and yet that nation till of late, made no great figure upon the ftage of the world. I am inclined to think that the territory of *Great Britain*, is more * valuable, though lefs extenfive,
than

midft of them; and how thefe farmers and their families, which he fuppofes to confift of 350 perfons, would bring to them and find maintenance for at leaft 1000 perfons more. The whole detail is too long for this place, and to abridge would be to maim it. This book was printed for C. *Rivington* in *St. Paul's Church-yard,* anno 1718.

* Befides having of our own growth, plenty of all forts of provifions, materials for buildings, apparel, &c we have alfo *lead, tin, copper, iron, calamy, coal, culm, allom, copperas, fullers earth,* and fundry other minerals; fome of which are in a manner the peculiar growth of this country, and very
defirable

than *France*; and the *Englijh* artifts upon
the whole, take the lead of all the world.
The *French* are much more numerous than
we are, and perhaps alfo more fkilful in
the arts of war ; and their government, for
fudden enterprifes, is * better framed than
ours : But the *Englijh* commonalty are more
robuft, brave and intrepid when roufed ;
and have from their foil and fkill in arts,
fuch great refources and advantages, that if
they do but preferve their † conftitution en-
tire, maintain a public fpirit, with union and
concord amongft themfelves; they may continue their independency upon other nations,
to the lateft times. But futurity is not ours.
Let us, whilft we are, each in his place, act
our parts like men, and all will be well.

The ftock of a nation in all forts of productions, natural and artificial, is to be included in the idea of its riches ; and more efpecially its ftock of thofe things that are neceffary
for the fupport of life, and for defence againft
enemies : For as men are circumftanced, this
last

defirable abroad : But I do not recollect to have heard, that
France yields any one natural product wanted by us.

* This advantage is, in many other refpects, much over-
balanced by the milder and more temperate frame of our
government.

† The freedom of this nation, is the true parent of its
grandeur : If ever it becomes enflaved, its auguft and
mighty monarch, will dwindle into an inconfiderable and
petty tyrant.

laft alfo is a neceffary ingredient. An induftrious and fkilful nation, having the land
well ftocked; the houfes well furnifhed; the
fhops, warehoufes, granaries and magazines
of all forts, well filled; may with great propriety be faid to be rich: To this eftimate,
muft be alfo added all the goods in foreign
warehoufes, that are the property of its merchants. When the riches of a country, are
confidered under this extenfive view; the
whole amount of its cafh or bullion, cannot
make fo confiderable a part, as people are
apt to imagine. We fhall confider more
particularly hereafter, in what fenfe, and
how far, gold and filver are riches: But we
are not to form an idea of the riches of
paft ages, from the abundance they had of
thofe metals. The *Inca's* of *Peru* were not
the richer, for the immenfe maffes of gold
they poffeffed; and its being fo greedily
coveted, proved the caufe of the lofs of their
country: Could they have changed their
gold into iron, it would have been vaftly
more ferviceable to them; and with it, they
might probably have defended their country,
againft thofe mercilefs invaders, that ufed
them fo barbaroufly. We fhould not yet
perhaps, reckon thofe people fo very defpi-
cable and poor, becaufe they had but few

of

of the arts amongft them: They were in poffeffion of a goodly country; had plenty of fuftenance; of fuch apparel and buildings, as gave them content: If they had no learning, they yet had good manners, probity, and a regular government; worthy, in many refpects, the imitation of the politeft *Europeans*. But we, having tafted the fweet fruits of arts, could not part with them, without feeling the utmoft reluctance; without being in a high degree fenfible of the calamitous diftreffes of poverty. It is in the product of arts, that riches chiefly confift; and if we reckon by this ftandard, the prefent age is probably richer than any of the paft; and our own nation is herein, not inferior to any of its neighbours.

Of fumptuary laws.

17. The defire of increafing in wealth and riches, is univerfal; many cry out againft luxury, and wifh to have it ftopped by *fumptuary laws*. But this is a matter of great delicacy, and requires a nice judgment: Such laws, if not well confidered, might be productive of effects, contrary to their intention. The curious arts of all forts, are beneficial to a country; and the difcouraging any of them, will, inftead of

beget-

2

begetting riches, bring on poverty. If men had contented themſelves with bare neceſſaries, we ſhould have wanted a thouſand conveniencies, which we now enjoy; and many of the talents given to us, would have been quite uſeleſs, for want of opportunities of exerting them. The word *luxury* hath uſually annexed to it, a kind of opprobrious idea; but ſo far as it encourages the arts, whets the inventions of men, and finds employments for more of our own people; its influence is benign, and beneficial to the whole ſociety. But if luxury, or faſhion, tend to diſcourage the arts and induſtry at home; to ſtock the nation too much with coſtly trifles from abroad, of no real uſe; or with conſumable commodities, not really wanted; thereby, transferring the employments from our own poor to thoſe of other nations; to nations, it may be, not our friends; luxury then, degenerates into evil, and ſhould be ſuppreſſed in time. Vanity, though it ruins many individuals, is yet perhaps beneficial to the community; and the ways of indulging it, ſhould not be too much ſtraightened : Prevent its leading to any intemperances, that may affect either the healths, morals, or induſtry of the people, and no harm will be done.

VI.

VI. *Induftry the fource of wealth, and good order that of induftry: Public fpirit the great fountain of national grandeur, and happinefs.*

18. I fhall conclude this chapter, with obferving again; that labour, fkill, and induftry, are the true fources of wealth; and the means of diftributing it, in a due proportion, among all the members of the body politic. It is not any fpecific quantity of money, but the due diftribution of it, that renders that body healthy and vigerous in all its parts. Idlenefs is the bane of fociety; the great fource of vice and confufion; the fore-runner of public diftrefs and calamity. Induftry produces the contrary effects; and is to be promoted by all poffible methods: Thefe are various; they are chiefly good laws, fpeedily, righteoufly, and cheaply executed; wife regulations of commerce, as well internal as foreign; good examples; a watchful care in the magiftrates, to fupprefs in the firft inftances, vice, floth, and all kinds of immoralities; a due care of the indigent and feeble, that none perifh for want, when there is more than fufficient for all; the fecuring of private property; a due difdain

2

dain of all chicanery, quibbling and fophi-
ftry, more efpecially, in fchools and courts
of juftice ; ability, uprightnefs and difpatch
in public offices ; the countenancing of probity, of plain dealing, of arts and fciences ;
and in all cafes, an inviolable maintenance of
public faith. Thefe, are fome of the ways,
to breed and cherifh a public fpirit, among
all ranks of people ; without which, no nation can be happy ; no community can long
fubfift.

A nation fkilful in arts, abounding in
products, untainted in its morals ; where
public fpirit prevails, above local and per-
fonal interefts ; and under a wife and righ-
teous government, duly tempered, fo as to
be fecure itfelf, and all under it fecure ; a
nation, I fay, under thefe circumftanees,
muft needs within itfelf, be rich, flourifh-
ing and happy. But power, grandeur, and
influence abroad, depend chiefly on the numbers of induftrious inhabitants at home. A
limited number, cannot acquire above a limited degree of wealth, or ftrength : The
way to increafe both, is to break down the
barricadoes of local enfranchifements ; to
encourage matrimony among the lower clafs,
by giving fome privileges to thofe who have
children ; finding employments for thofe
who

who are able; and fupplying with neceffaries, the helplefs and indigent. Moreover, if
you pleafe, you may invite hither foreign Pro-
teftants; by giving the privileges of free de-
nifons, to all that are defirous of incorporat-
ing themfelves under the banner of our laws,
and enjoying the benefits of our happy conftitution. But fome better regulations fhould
be made with regard to our own poor, before ftrangers can be induced to come a-
mong us.

D   C H A P-

C H A P T E R II.
Of M O N E Y, *and* C O I N S.

I. *Of Barter.*

19. T H E firſt commerce amongſt men, was undoubtedly carried on by *barter*, or the exchange of one commodity for another ; and indeed, this is the true and ultimate end of all commerce, whether foreign or domeſtic. But as men and arts increaſed, a mere barter of commodities became inconvenient, and inſufficient, in abundance of inſtances. For it muſt needs frequently happen, that one man would want goods of another, that wanted none at the preſent, of thoſe goods which he had to give him in exchange ; and therefore to him, theſe goods would be but of ſmall value ; and it might be a tedious and intricate courſe, before the goods of the firſt man could be ſo often bartered, till at length they became exchanged into that particular commodity, which the ſecond wanted. The ſame inconvenience would attend private bills, or promiſſory notes ; for the *note* could not well be

be difcharged, till the man who gave it, met with a cuftomer, that had goods which fuited him, to whom the faid note had been given. Add to this, that contracts payable in goods were uncertain; for goods even of the fame kind, differ in value. One horfe is worth more than another horfe: Wheat off one field, is better than wheat off another. Cows, horfes, fwine, &c. wheat, barley, oats, &c. might differ greatly in their value; a great difparity alfo would frequently happen, between artificial things of the fame fort, as one workman excelled another. So that in this ftate of barter, befides the endlefs difficulties people were under to fuit one another; there was no fcale, or meafure, by which the proportion of value which goods had to one another, could be afcertained *.

D 2   II.

* In a ftate of barter, there can be but little trade, and few artizans. For want of a ready exchange for their goods, people would look little farther than to get food, and fome coarfe raiment: The landed men would till only fo much land, as fufficed their own families; and to procure them thofe few rude neceffaries, which the country afforded. Hence, without fome kind of money, the arts can make no progrefs; and without the arts, a country cannot flourifh or grow populous. Ignorance and idlenefs will naturally beget trefpaffes, incroachments, wars and contentions, ever deftructive to the growth of people. Does not this account for what we daily fee, even amongft nations reckoned polite? And how important is it, that the rulers of the earth fhould be more liberally educated?

II. MONEY, *what, and whence it arose.*

20. To avoid the great inconveniencies of mere barter, a material or commodity that should be universally accepted in exchange for all other things, was soon agreed upon; and this is what we call * MONEY. As soon

as

* The first step from mere barter to the invention of money, was probably by *pledges* or deposites, which the owner was to redeem. And metals being durable, divisible without loss, and easy of carriage; and having from their usefulness a value set upon them, like other things; men coveted to have metals for their pledges, and some one metal, preferable to the rest; and this desire becoming universal, that metal, from being used as a mere pledge, soon became money. Suppose this metal was silver: " He who had " more goods than he had occasion for, would chuse to bar- " ter them for silver, though he had no use for it; because " silver would not decay upon his hands, or be of any ex- " pence to him in keeping; and with it he could purchase " other goods as he had occasion, in whole or in part, at " home or abroad; silver being divisible without loss, and " of the same value in different places. *Ex.* If *A* had " 100 sheep, and desired to exchange them for horses: *B* " had 10 horses, which were equal to, or worth the 100 " sheep, and was willing to exchange: But *A* not having " present occasion for the horses, rather than be at the ex- " pence of keeping them, he would barter his sheep with *C*, " who had the value to give in silver, with which he could " purchase the horses at the time he had occasion. Or, if " *C* had not silver, but was willing to give his bond for the " silver, or the horses, payable at the time *A* wanted them: " *A* would chuse to take the bond payable in silver, rather " than in horses; because silver was certain in quality, and " horses differed much. So silver was used as the value in " which contracts were made payable." And thus the transitions from *bartering* to *pledging*, and from *pledges* to *money*, were very natural and obvious.

The above extract is taken from an ingenious piece, tho' not free from some grievous mistakes, of the celebrated Mr. *John Law's*, entitled, *Money and trade considered*, printed at *London* in 1720.

as this invention became eftablifhed, men
reckoned the value of their goods by money; and the terms *prices, buying,* and *fell-
ing* came in ufe; a greater or lefs quantity
of money going to the purchafe of all things,
in proportion to the refpective values which
before had been fet upon them, as well in
refpect of that commodity now made money, as of one another.

Thus, MONEY *is a* STANDARD MEASURE,
*by which the values of all things, are regu-
lated and afcertained; and is it felf, at the
fame time, the* VALUE *or* EQUIVALENT, *by
which, goods are exchanged, and in which,
contracts are made payable.* So that money,
is not a pledge, to be afterwards redeemed;
but is both an equivalent and a meafure;
being in all contracts, the very thing ufually bargained for, as well as the meafure of
the bargain : Or, if one thing be bartered
for another ; the meafure of the bargain, is
ufually the quantity of money, which each
of the things bartered, are conceived to be
worth.

To illuftrate this fubject farther, let us
fuppofe *filver* to be that commodity, which
was fixed upon as money. Silver had before a known value, from its ufes as a metal ; and being durable, portable, divifible

D 3   with-

without lofs, and of equal goodnefs every
where, as will be explained hereafter, was
found every way convenient for the purpofe
of money ; and having been applied to that
ufe, filver received an additional value to
that which it had before, as a mere metal,
from the greater demand for it thence arifing. As foon as filver was made money,
it was ufed, both as the value in which contracts were made payable, and alfo as the meafure, by which goods were valued; and confequently, of the proportion of value of different
goods to one another. Thus, as Mr. *Locke*
obferves, " the value of lead to wheat, for
" inftance, and of either of them to a cer-
" tain fort of cloth, is known by the prices
" of each, or their value in filver or mo-
" ney. As if a yard of cloth be worth or
" fells for half an ounce of filver, a bufhel
" of wheat for one ounce, and a hundred
" weight of lead for two ounces ; any one
" prefently fees and fays, that a bufhel of
" wheat is double the value of a yard of
" that cloth, and but half the value of an
" hundred weight of lead." And according to thefe proportions, any quantity of the
above commodities will exchange, either
for money, or for one another. So that, as
before obferved, money is always the ftandard

dard that * meafures the values of commodities ; and, moft commonly, is alfo what is
given for them, or the equivalent with or
for which they are purchafed.

*How money differs from other meafures, and
alfo from commodities.*

21. In the idea of money, the quality
of the material is fuppofed to be unchange-
able, and to be univerfally or every where
the fame : And therefore, the material being
once fixed or agreed upon; all that is to be
included in the idea of money, is the quantity only of that material, as in other ftandard meafures, whether of weight or extenfion : And the only effential difference betwixt them, is this; that money is not only a
meafure, but alfo an equivalent, and as fuch
paffes from one to another ; whilft other

D 4   meafures,

* In like manner, money is ufed as the meafure by
which goods to be delivered in different places, are valued.
Ex. If a piece of wine was to be delivered at *London* by *A,*
merchant there, to the order of *B,* vintner at *Brecknock*;
and the value to be delivered in butter at *Brecknock,* by *B*
to the order of *A.* The wine is not be valued by the
quantity of butter it is worth at *London,* nor the butter
by the quantity of wine it is worth at *Brecknock.* The
way to know what quantity of butter is equal to the wine,
is, by the quantity of money, each is worth at the places
where they are to be delivered : Thus, fuppofing as before,
filver to be money ; if the piece of wine be worth at *London* 20 ounces of filver, and 20 ounces of filver be worth
14 ftones of butter at *Brecknock*; then 24 ftones is the quantity of butter to be given there, in return for the wine.

meafures, may reft indifferently in the buyer's or feller's, or a third perfon's hands, it matters not whofe they be.

Money alfo differs from all commodities in this, that, as fuch, its value is permanent or unalterable; that is, money being the meafure of the values of all other things, and that, like all other ftandard meafures, by its quantity only; its own value is to be deemed invariable: And all contracts or engagements, are to be deemed fully difcharged and fatisfied, by the payment of the fpecific quantity or fum of money, agreed upon; without having any regard to the value of money, with refpect to other things, at the different times of contracting and difcharging of debts.

This is a fundamental characteriftic of money, without which, it would lofe its ufe as fuch; nor can money, with any propriety, be confidered as being fubject to vary in its value, without referring it to fomething elfe as a ftandard; and thereby, departing from its ufe as money, and making it a mere commodity.

Of fome requifite properties in the material of money.

22. That money may continue in efteem, and preferve the public eftimation, as an
equi-

equivalent, and a standard meafure; it is necessary that it be made of a material or commodity, which is not too common, not too cheap or bulky, not growing fpontaneoufly, or to be found without a valuable confideration in labour or land; not very fubject to be confumed with ufe, or to be fpoiled for the want of ufe, nor fubject to expence in keeping. For money, like other things, whatever pains may be taken to fhew, or fome may think to the contrary; will foon find a value, in proportion to the labour and fkill, that are neceffary to acquire it; or in a reciprocal proportion to its plenty. Though we reckon by money; yet labour and fkill, are the main * ftandards, by which, the values of all or moft things are ultimately afcertained; and there will require a greater or lefs bulk of money, to purchafe the very fame thing, according as there is a greater or lefs quantity of money in circulation; that is, according as the material of money is cheaper or dearer, or in greater or leffer plenty.

The ufe of money is very general, as well as antient; and many poor ftates, that had fcarce any arts or traffic amongft them, had

yet

* Art. 7.

yet a fort of money. In fome parts of *Africa*,
the fmall fhells called by us *couries*, paffed
as money ; and in fome other parts of that
barbarous continent, *falt*, being very fcarce,
and therefore much valued, was ufed as
money : In the one place, a certain number
of fhells ; and in the other, a certain meafure or weight of falt ; going to the purchafe
of fuch and fuch a commodity.   But among
trading and polite nations, fuch common
materials or commodities, would not do for
money ; their money muft be fuch as hath
an intrinfic value, and thence, an univerfal
efteem among thofe they traffic with.

A nation fecluded from the reft of the
world, might indeed, fall upon various methods of fupplying the ufe of money : And
we fee that fome of our plantations, make
a fhift without any money, properly fo called ; ufing only bits of ftamped paper, of
no real value.   But, wherever that material, which paffeth as or inftead of money,
hath no intrinfic value, arifing from its ufefulnefs, fcarcity, and neceffary expence of
labour in procuring it ; there, private property will be precarious ; and fo long as
that continues to be the cafe, it will be
next to impoffible for fuch people, to ar-
                                                        rive

rive at any great degree of power and fplendor *.

Metals, the fitteft materials of money.

23. For the purpofe of univerfal commerce, metals feem the fitteft materials for a ftandard meafure, or *money*; as *copper*, *filver*, or *gold*; they having all the properties above required : They are moreover divifible into minute parts, which parts retain neverthelefs an intrinfic value, in proportion to their quantity or weight ; becaufe thofe parts may, without injuring the metal, be again united together into a greater mafs. Thefe metals are durable, and alfo
fufceptible

* There is a very wide and effential difference, betwixt money and bills : The one, having an intrinfic value, is in all contracts and dealings, the equivalent, as well as the meafure. Bills are nothing, but mere promifes or obligations of payment : And even public bills, for fuch only ufually pafs as money, have only a local credit, being limited to the territories of the ftate that iffued them ; and depending merely upon their faith, thofe that are in private hands are, to fay no worfe, fubject every day to be debafed by the creation of more new bills. For bills, whilft they pafs as money, partake fo far of its nature, that the more, or for a greater fum, there are of them in currency, the lefs will be the value of any given bill, or a bill for a given fum.
  Some of our plantations, have feverely felt the ill effects of thofe weak, unjuft and deftructive meafures, of increafing the quantities of bills ; whilft the *Philadelphians*, by keeping facredly to a certain number or fum total of bills, have not only preferved their credit amongft themfelves ; but even extended it, to fome of the neighbouring provinces ; where, I am informed, a *Philadelphian* bill will fetch more than one of their own, made for the fame or a like fum.

fufceptible of any form, mark, or impref-
fion; and are convertible from money or
coins, into utenfils of various kinds; and
from thefe, into money again. Thefe properties are what give money, which is generally made of one or other of the above
metals, a real and intrinfic value. There is
fcarce room to imagine, that money, made
of a material good for no other purpofe,
would long continue in efteem, as fuch; the
ufefulnefs and fcarcity of the materials, are
both confidered in the common eftimation
of money.

Bafe metals not fit materials of money.

24. Again, it is requifite that that metal
which is made money, or the ftandard meafure of commerce, fhould be either of equal
goodnefs every where, according to its quantity or weight; or, that there fhould be
fome certain criterion, by which might be
afcertained, the true proportional value of
any given mafs of that metal, when compared with any other given mafs of the
fame metal. Money cannot be a proper or
exact meafure of the values of other things,
if its own value is queftionable; for if it
could be doubted, whether my ounce of
money, be precifely of the fame value with
                                          any

any other perfon's ounce of money; it would create fuch a diftraction in all kinds of traffic, that would fruftrate the very end and defign of money.

The *bafe metals*, as *copper*, *tin*, *lead*, and *iron*, have none of them the above quality, or that precife certainty of value, required in money. For, although the artifts employed about them, can foon find that this mafs of copper, for inftance, is better or worfe than that other mafs, at leaft for their particular purpofes ; yet, there is no method of afcertaining, to any exactnefs, what is their refpective purenefs ; or what is the fpecific difference betwixt, or what is the true proportional value of, different maffes of that metal in refpect of one another. And therefore * copper, is not a fit material for money : And the other bafe metals, are ftill more unfit ; for the like, and other reafons, that are fufficiently obvious. Their great plenty and cheapnefs, is a farther objection to the making money of any of the bafer metals.

III.

---

* Copper coins with us are properly not money, but a kind of *tokens* paffing by way of exchange inftead of parts of the fmalleft pieces of filver coin ; and as fuch, very ufeful in fmall home traffic.

III. *Fine silver and fine gold, of equal goodness every where.*

25. Silver and gold, when pure and unmixed with base metals, are called *fine*, or *fine silver*, and *fine gold*. And thefe, calle'd the *precious* and *noble metals*, when thus pure, have every where the fame characteriftics, and in all refpects the fame qualities, fo far as hath hitherto been difcovered ; that is, an ounce of any fine filver, is exactly of the fame intrinfic worth or value, with an ounce of any other fine filver: And the fame of fine gold, with refpect to fine gold.

But thefe precious metals, are feldom found pure, till they are made fo by art for particular purpofes ; and when they are not pure, the metal commixed with them is called *alloy*. This alloy is reckoned of no value ; that is, if to an ounce of fine filver be fuperadded, fuppofe, an ounce of copper ; this addition of copper, though it increafes the mafs to double the quantity, yet gives that mafs no additional value : So that one ounce of fine filver, is of as * great value

---

* A certain proportion of copper will even depreciate the value of the filver mixed with it ; if this proportion be fo great, as to make the filver not fit for common purpofes, without refining.

value as the two ounces of this mixed mafs. And the reafon of it is, becaufe thefe metals cannot be again feparated, either without a total lofs of the copper, or without more coft than profit. In like manner, not only copper, but filver alfo, is an alloy to gold ; and when they are commixed together, the filver is reckoned of no value, unlefs it be in fuch proportion to the gold, as to make it worth the refiner's while to feparate them *.

Silver and gold, when alloyed, are faid to be of fuch a finenefs, according to the proportion there is of fine filver or fine gold, to the whole mafs. Thus, a mafs of filver, containing eleven parts of pure or fine filver, and one part of alloy, is faid to be $\frac{11}{12}$ fine ; or with us in *England*, eleven ounces fine ; becaufe our pound for weighing gold and filver, is fubdivided into twelve ounces.

IV.

* For the fame reafon, a proportion even of gold mixed with filver, that is lefs than a penny weight in a pound Troy, doth not add to the value of the filver, excepting fo far as it increafes the mafs ; the gold, in this cafe, being reckoned only as filver, and not confidered as increafing the value of that filver, with which it is mixed. And I am informed, that a penny weight of gold in a pound weight of filver, is the leaft proportion of gold, that will pay for refining ; this being reckoned a profit only, of about one farthing *per* ounce.

IV. *Silver and gold the only proper and fit*
materials of money.

26. The degrees of finenefs of both filver and gold, are difcoverable, by fkilful
affay-mafters, to great exactnefs ; and thefe
metals, being univerfally of equal goodnefs,
according to their purity, they are proper
materials of money. And indeed, they have
manifeftly a peculiar fitnefs for that purpofe, above any other material hitherto
known ; and accordingly, thefe metals only
are ufed as fuch, by all the polite and trading nations of the world.

V. *Of* C o i n s.

27. As the intrinfic qualities, or degrees
of finenefs of given maffes of filver and
gold, are not difcoverable without art, trouble and expence ; the expediency of coining was foon difcovered. The public ftamp
upon coins, is a voucher and fecurity to
every one, that the coins that wear it, are
of a certain finenefs, and intrinfic value, according to their fize or weight : And coins
alfo, being more diftributive than bullion,
are, upon that account likewife, more convenient for trade, and in the common affairs
of life.

Names

Names of coins, and of integral sums of money, taken chiefly from weights.

28. In antient times, the names of given sums of money, do not seem to have been properly the names of any species of coin, but of different proportions of weights : As the *talent, sheckle, mina, drachma,* &c. and in later times, *pound, mark,* &c. The mark is now difused by us; but in several of the neighbouring countries, it is still their integer for weighing metals, and is subdivided into eight ounces. And when the art of coining became established, the coins took their names from certain weights, used in the respective countries; to which weights, the coins at first exactly corresponded. The integral sums of money, were also denominated, from integral weights; as the *livre* in *France,* and the *pound* in *England* and *Scotland*; and so many of the coins as made the *sum* of one pound, or a *money* pound, made also exactly a pound in *weight.* At present, we have only the names *pound* and *penny,* that are common both to money and weights : Antiently, a *shilling* was here the name of a given weight; and 240 pennies made the *sum,* as at present, of one

E   pound

pound, and a pound weight. But now, a
filver penny is only the $\frac{10}{11}$ of a penny-weight
Troy; which is a little more, than a third
of what a penny weighed at the conqueſt.

Of our preſent weights, and diviſions of money.

29. It is thought that the *livre*, or pound
weight, of filver, was inſtituted as the *money integer*, by CHARLEMAGNE : And this
he ſubdivided into *ſols*, and *deniers*, which
bore exactly the ſame proportion to the
pound, as our *ſhillings* and *pence*, now do,
to our *money pound*, or *pound ſterling*. I
have not met with any diſtinct account of
the *Saxon* weights; but it is very probable,
that the weight called the *pound of the Tower
of London*, was the old *Saxon pound*. This
pound contained $11\frac{1}{4}$ ounces Troy; and did
not very ſenſibly differ, from 12 ounces of
the weight ſtill uſed in the money affairs of
Germany; and there known, by the name
of *Colonia* weight. The *Tower weight* continued in uſe at the mint there, from the
conqueſt till the 18th year of the reign of
Henry VIII; at which time it was laid aſide,
and the *Troy weight* introduced in its ſtead.
The *Saxon* or *Tower pound weight*, was divided,

vided, as our *money pound* now is, into *ſhillings*, *pennies* and *farthings*; and it ſeems very probable that antiently, the weights anſwering to theſe names and ſubdiviſions, were thoſe in common uſe.

I was obliged to my late learned friend MARTIN FOLKES, Eſq; for this account of the *Saxon* weight, &c. long before he publiſhed his curious *Table of Engliſh ſilver coins*, where the ſame is to be met with: A work which none, who are deſirous of having an exact hiſtory of our coins, ſhould be without; and from which, as a farther illuſtration of this ſubject, I beg leave to make the * following extract.

The

* *Page* 1, 2. The Troy weight, *Pondus Trecenſe*, from *Troyes* in *Champagne*, is generally ſuppoſed to have been introduced here by the *Normans*; but does not ſeem to have been immediately eſtabliſhed. It is moſt probable that the pound of the *Tower*, or the monyers pound, was alſo the pound in common uſe before the conqueſt; and that it continued to be ſo for a conſiderable time after, till the Troy pound, perhaps from its greater weight, got the preference by degrees. It is obſervable, that in the old ſtatute called *Aſſiſa panis & cereviſiæ*, 51 *Hen.* III. and which it ſelf refers to " older ordinances made in the time of the king's proge-" nitors," the weights of the ſeveral quantities of bread, &c. therein mentioned, are not expreſſed in Troy but in money weights, that is, in pounds, ſhillings, pennies, and farthings. " When a quarter of wheat is ſold for xii *d.* then " waſtel breade of a ferthing ſhall weigh vi *li.* and xvi *s.* " Breade cocket of a ferthing of the ſame corne and bultel, " ſhall weigh more than waſtel by ii *s.* Cocket breade made " of corne that is of leſs price, ſhall weigh more than waſ-" tel by v *s.* A ſimnel of a ferthing ſhall weigh ii *s.* leſs " than waſtel, &c."

Our

*That coins in all or moſt countries have, at
   different times, been debaſed; but the ſame
   denominations ſtill continued.*

30. The antient denominations given to
money, in the ſeveral countries, have been
ſtill continued; but the coins which made
up the ſums ſo denominated, have been
ſince, at different times, greatly debaſed or
diminiſhed in their value *. And now coins,

are

Our learned author goes on, and brings ſeveral more
authorities to ſhew, that the money or *Tower* weights, known
alſo in *France*, were thoſe antiently uſed in *England*. But I
ſhall treſpaſs no farther upon him here, than in adding the following extract of a *verdict relating to the coinage of 30th Octob.*
18 *Hen.* VIII, remaining in the Receipt of the Exchequer at
Weſtminſter, in which are the following words. " And whereas
" heretofore the merchaunte paid for coynage of every
" pounde *Towre* of fyne gold, weighing xi oz. quarter
" Troye, ii *s.* vi *d.* Nowe it is determyned by the king's
" highneſs, and his ſaid councelle, that the foreſaid pounde
" *Towre*, ſhall be no more uſed and occupied, but al maner
" of golde and ſylver ſhall be wayed by the pounde Troye,
" which exceedith the pounde *Towre* in weight iii quarters
" of the oz."
   The above citation ſhews the preciſe time when the
Tower or old *Saxon weight*, was laid aſide, *viz.* 30th
Octob. 1527; and that the proportion of the *Tower* pound
to the Troy pound, was exactly as 15 to 16.
   * Our money pound is at preſent only $\frac{10}{29.5833}$, or about
one-third, of what it was at the conqueſt; for then it contained $11\frac{1}{4}$ ounces of our preſent Troy weight, and now it
is $\frac{20}{61}$ of a Troy pound. By this rule, the readers of
Mr. *Lowndes* and of ſome other authors, may correct the
accounts which he gives of our coins. At the acceſſion of
King *James* I. to this throne, the *Scotch money pound* was
but equal to the $\frac{1}{12}$ of ours; and the *French livre* is at preſent, only about half the value of the *Scotch pound*.

are fo far from being ferviceable as weights,
which they once were; that, with us, as well
as in the neigbouring countries, the weight
of each piece is not readily known; being
very different, from any of the weights in
common ufe.

The original ftandards of coins, having
been once impaired; and the fame names
ftill remaining, after the fubftance had been
diminifhed, people did not know where to
ftop; and they feem to have thought, that
coins had their value, fome how, from the
ftamp they bore. And hence, for no better reafon can be affigned, fprang thofe
* adulterations of the coins, and the diftrac-
tions and complaints confequent thereupon,
that are to be met with in the hiftories of
moft countries.

VI. *Standard of monies.*

31. *Coins* being fo very convenient, they
only, are commonly confidered and ufed,
as *money*; whilft *bullion*, or gold and filver
unwrought and unftamped, are reckoned
mere commodities. And in all countries,
there is eftablifhed a certain *ftandard*, both

E 3   as

* The *Englifh*, to their great honour, have adulterated
their coins lefs than moft of their neighbours. A fum-
mary account of thefe adulterations with us, will be given
hereafter.

as to finenefs and weight, of the feveral
fpecies of their coins. In *England*, the filver monies are to contain 111 parts of fine
filver, and 9 parts alloy; and 62 of thofe
coins called fhillings, are to weigh a pound
Troy: That is, the pound Troy with us,
contains 11 ounces 2 penny-weights of fine
filver, and 18 penny-weights of alloy; and
of a pound Troy of this ftandard filver, our
money pound called the *pound* * *fterling*,
contains $\frac{20}{62}$ parts; or the pound fterling is
$= \frac{20}{62}$ of $\frac{11}{12}$ of a pound Troy of fine filver. And this ftandard hath continued with
us invariably, ever fince the 43d year of
the reign of Queen *Elizabeth*.

The ftandard of our prefent gold coins,
is 11 parts of fine gold, and 1 part of alloy; and $44\frac{1}{2}$ guineas are cut out of a pound
Troy; fo that a guinea is $= \frac{1}{44\frac{1}{2}}$ of 11
ounces of fine gold. The finenefs of gold
is not with us, reckoned by the common
weights, but by imaginary ones, called † *ca-*
rats: The higheft degree of finenefs, or

pure

* The filver monies of *England*, are now known by the
name of *fterling* or *fterling money*: A name fuppofed to be
derived from fome *Netherlanders*, who were formerly here
employed in coining money, and then called here *Eaflerlings*.

† Mr. *Roberts*, in his *map of commerce*, page 24, 199,
takes notice, that at *Venice* they have a real weight called
carat; whence we had the name *carat*, and alfo the weight

pure gold, is called 24 carats; fo that our
ftandard is 22 carats of fine gold, and 2 carats of alloy.   The carats are fubdivided
into 4 parts called *grains*, and thefe again
into quarters; fo that a *carat grain*, with
refpect to the common divifions of a pound
Troy, is equivalent to $2\frac{1}{2}$ penny-weights.

The ftandard of money farther explained.

32. It is carefully to be remembered, that
by the *ftandard of money*, is always meant,
the quantity of pure or fine metal contained
in a given fum; and not merely the degree
of purity or finenefs of that metal; but the
finenefs and grofs weight are both included.
Thus, the ftandard of a pound fterling, is
3 oz. 11 dwt. $14\frac{22}{31}$ grains Troy of fine filver; which is equal to 3 oz. 17 dwt. $10\frac{2}{3}$ gr.
of filver 11 oz. 2 dwt. fine, which is our
ftandard of finenefs.   The ftandard of a
fhilling, is $73\frac{22}{31}$ grains Troy of fine filver,
or $80\frac{28}{31}$ grains of filver $\frac{11}{12}$ fine.

E 4   The

fo called by jewellers; and that the *Venetians* had this weight
from the *Indians* or *Moors*.   This author fays, that 150 *Venetian* carats, make one ounce Troy; fo that one carat is
equal to $3\frac{1}{5}$ grains Troy, which is nearly the weight of the
carat ufed by our jewellers.   The late learned and curious
MARTIN FOLKES, Efq; found by a nice examination when
he was at *Venice*, that a *Venetian* carat doth weigh as above,
or that 150 of thofe carats do make pretty exactly one ounce
Troy.

The ſtandard of our money, ſtrictly ſpeaking, remains the ſame, ſo long as there is the ſame quantity of pure ſilver in the reſpective coins having the old or given denominations; though the coins may be varied, by making them, either of finer ſilver and lighter, or of coarſer ſilver and heavier. But ſuch deviations from the old method of coining, would be imprudent; as it might create ſuſpicion of ſome unfair dealings, and would anſwer no good purpoſe. On the other hand, the ſtandard may be debaſed or lowered, either by coining the ſeveral ſpecies lighter, but of the old fineneſs; or by retaining the old weights, and making them of coarſer ſilver; or without altering the reſpective coins, by making a ſmaller number of them go to the *pound ſterling*, which is our *Unit* or money ſtandard. And by debaſing the ſtandard, I every where mean, the leſſening of the quantity of pure ſilver in the pound ſterling, or in the reſpective ſpecie which by law is ordained to make up that ſum; without regarding the particular manner, in or by which, this may be done.

Why

Why coins and plate have alloy.

33. As the alloy mixed with filver and gold, is reckoned of no value; it may be afked, why any alloy is put into coins, and plate? The reafons are thefe: 1. It is feldom or ever, that filver or gold, are found pure in the mines; and the trouble of refining to make them fo, would be very great and expenfive: And 2. a certain proportion of alloy, renders thefe metals harder, and fitter for the ufes, to which they are commonly applied. The ftandard of about $\frac{11}{12}$ fine, is very convenient: For, if it be much coarfer, both filver and gold will lofe of their colour, beauty, and ductility; and if the ftandard be much finer; thofe metals will be too foft for many purpofes, and a great expence of refining will be unavoidable.

VII. *There can be but one ftandard of money.*

34. Hitherto, we have confidered both filver and gold, as being either of them a fit material to be made, or ufed as money. But although there may be good reafons for coining each of them; yet it is very certain, that one only of thefe metals can be the

money,

money, or *ſtandard meaſure of commerce*, in
any country. For the ſtandard meaſure
muſt be invariable, and keep the ſame proportion of value, in all its parts: Such is
ſilver with reſpect to ſilver, and gold to
gold; that is, an ounce of ſilver is always
worth juſt an ounce of ſilver; and two
ounces of the one or the other of theſe metals, is juſt double the value of one ounce
of the ſame. But ſilver and gold, with reſpect to one another, are, like other commodities, variable in their value; according
as the plenty of either, may be increaſed
or diminiſhed; and an ounce of gold that
is worth a given quantity of ſilver to-day,
may be worth more or leſs ſilver, a while
hence. And therefore it is impoſſible, that
both theſe metals, can be a ſtandard meaſure of the values of other things, at the
ſame time; and one of them muſt be a
mere commodity, with reſpect to the other.

*Silver the money or ſtandard meaſure of
the greateſt part, if not of all* Europe.

35. Silver coin is, and time immemorial
hath been, the money of accompt of the
greateſt part of the world; and in all countries where it is ſo, *ſilver* is truly the *ſtandard*

3   *mea-*

meafure of commerce; and all other metals, gold as well as lead, are but commodities rateable by filver.

In *England*, accounts are kept or reckoned by the *pound ſterling*; which, as hath been before obferved, is a certain quantity of fine filver appointed by law for a ftandard. It is according to this ftandard, that the public revenues are eftablifhed; lands are let; falaries, ftipends, and wages fettled; and univerfally, all forts of contracts both public and private, are made and governed by this ftandard. And altho' it be fuppofed, that with us, more payments, or of greater value, are made in gold than in filver coins; yet that doth not alter the ftandard, whilft the accounts are kept in filver; fo long, in all our internal dealings at leaft, the gold can be only a commodity, fuppofed to be worth fo much filver as it paffeth for *: And the cafe would be the fame, although our filver coins fhould grow yet fcarcer.

VIII. *Silver the fitteſt material, hitherto known, for money.*

36. All nations having, for fo many ages, made ufe of filver for the ftandard meafure

of

* This whole matter relating to the ftandard of our money, fhall be farther difcuffed hereafter.

of the values of other things; that alone,
seems to be a sufficient reason for continuing the same standard; and the altering it
now, from silver to gold, was the thing it
self practicable, would beget great perplexities in all kinds of dealings and accompts.
But farther, silver being of a more moderate
value than gold, is, * for that reason, better suited for the purpose of money. For
the integer and its several parts, should bear
an exact and due proportion of value to
each other; and this would be impossible,
if they were made of different materials.
There must be coins of about the values of
shillings, and six-pences; and it would be
better, if we had some that were still
smaller: Those sorts of coins are the most
frequently wanted; and there is no doing
without them, or some substitutes in their
stead. But these substitutes, being made
of a different material from the standard
money, are not themselves to be reckoned
money; for the using such, would be a deviation from the true use and intent of money;

---

* It is also for the same reason, better suited for the making of various sorts of utensils; and money, as hath been
before observed, is intrinsically valuable because, by melting, the material is convertible into something useful. And
it may be questioned, whether coins had preserved their
value, and been continued as money, if silver and gold had
not been applicable to other purposes.

ney ; and would fubject the people where
they paffed, to loffes and perplexities. A
coin of a fhilling, or even of half a crown
value, would be too fmall in gold ; and
therefore at prefent, gold is much too valuable for a ftandard of money. And it
would be a ridiculous and vain attempt, to
make a ftandard integer of gold, whofe
parts fhould be filver ; or to make a motly
ftandard, part gold and part filver. Thefe
different materials could not long agree in
value ; and filver being the moft common
and ufeful coin, would foon regain its antient place of a *ftandard meafurer*.

Silver, I think, is lefs fubject to variation in its value, than gold. For filver
having been diftributed in great quantities
over all *Europe*, as well in coin as in plate
of various forts ; a fudden influx, or efflux
of it, by a quicker or flower production of
the mines, doth not fo foon affect the whole
mafs. The wages of day-labour, being
alfo ufually paid in filver, may be another
great reafon, of a more even and permanent value of this metal. But without laying much ftrefs, upon the greater variations in the value of gold ; which perhaps
may be alfo partly owing, to its being every
where in the eyes of the laws a mere commodity ;

modity; I think, it is fufficiently evident
that filver at prefent, is a much fitter ftandard to meafure with, than gold.

Silver a fit ftandard, though its plenty varies.

37. It may be here objeＣted, that as the
value of filver, like all other commodities,
muft needs be variable, according as the
plenty of it is increafed or diminifhed; filver
cannot be a * fixed ftandard, like that of
mere extenfion as a yard or a bufhel, for
mea-

* Mr. LOCKE well obferves, that that grain which is the
moft conftant and general food of any country, as *wheat* in
England, and *rice* in *Turkey*, is the moft likely thing to keep
the fame proportion to its vent for a long courfe of time;
and therefore the fitteft thing to referve a rent in, which is
defigned to be conftantly the fame in all future ages; and
the fitteft meafure whereby to judge of the altered values of
things in any long traＣt of time. For in *England*, and in
this part of the world, wheat being the conftant and moft
general food, not altering with the fafhion, not growing by
chance; but as the farmers fow more or lefs of it, which
they endeavour to proportion, as near as can be gueffed, to
the confumption; it muft needs fall out that it keeps the
neareft proportion to its confumption, (which is more ftudied
and defigned in this than other commodities) of any thing,
if you take it for feven or twenty years together: Though
perhaps the plenty or fcarcity of one year, caufed by the
accidents of the feafon, may very much vary it from the
immediately precedent or following, But wheat, or any
other grain, cannot ferve inftead of money; becaufe of its
bulkinefs, and too quick change of its quantity. For had
I a bond to pay me 100 bufhels of wheat next year, it
might be a fourth part lofs or gain to me; too great an in-
equality, to be ventured in trade: Befides the different goodnefs of feveral parcels of wheat in the fame year. But money is the beft meafure of the altered value of things in a
few years; becaufe its vent is the fame, and its quantity
alters but flowly. *Locke's works, vol.* II. p. 23, 24.

meafuring the values of other things.   It probably cannot; and perhaps filver is now quantity for quantity, of three or four times lefs value, than it was two or three centuries ago.   But yet, filver being durable, well known, efteemed, diftributed in confiderable quantities over all *Europe*; and its growth, plenty, goodnefs or intrinfic qualities, not immediately depending upon feafons of weather and other cafualties; the alteration of its value hath been, for the moft part, gradual; and is not likely hereafter to be very confiderable of a fudden, though it may in a long courfe of time.   And therefore, filver is as good a ftandard meafure or money, as the prefent ftate of things will admit of; and very fit and ufeful to be continued as fuch.

We are at prefent but little concerned, with what might be the value of filver in former times; and as little, with what may be its value hereafter.   The prices of things will naturally conform to the ftandard, whilft the alterations in it are flow and gradual, and not forced.   But, from the nature of things, the proportion of money to goods, is ever fubject to fome variations; and all that can be done, to prevent the inconveniencies that might thence arife, is to limit contracts within a moderate term of years:

For,

For, in contracts, quantity only is to be confidered; and no regard can be had to the
future value of money, without deviating
entirely from its ufe as fuch, and rendering
all contracts uncertain.

IX. *Gold coins fhould pafs as money.*

38. Although filver is the only ftandard
meafure of all our contracts; yet gold having every other quality fitting it for money,
excepting its being too dear; it may be very
fit and ufeful to coin gold, to afcertain its
finenefs; and to let.thefe coins pafs in lieu
of money, at fome * given rate: For gold
coins are very convenient, in large payments.   But it fhould not be faid or underftood, that a *guinea*, for inftance, fhould be
always an equivalent for the fame quantity
of filver.   For as gold, like other commodities, muft be ever fubject to alter in its
value, with refpect to filver; the price of this
dazzling metal can be no otherwife fettled,
                                    than

---

* As there can be but one ftandard of money, and filver
is and ought to be that ftandard; Mr. *Locke* was, and others
are, of the opinion, that gold coins fhould be left to find
their own value, without having any eftablifhed legal rates.
But this is a matter, I think, of too much importance to
be entrufted to private judgment; and, if left at large,
might fubject the nation in general to great impofitions,
by a combination of the traders in coins.   But of this fubject, and alfo of copper coins, more hereafter.

3

than *pro tempore*. And in all contracts, the price of gold at the time of payment is only to be confidered; and not what price it might bear, at the times when the contracts were made.

X. *Of* TOKENS, *or bafe coins.*

39. Although filver, bulk for bulk, is now about 26 times cheaper than gold; yet filver is too dear to be coined into fpecie of the lowest denominations of our money. A filver penny is too fmall for common ufe; and yet pence, and their halfs, and quarters, enter daily into accounts. To fupply the want of very fmall filver coins, a kind of TOKENS or fubftitutes have been inftituted; thefe, are now with us, all made of copper, and of two fpecies only, called *halfpence*, and *farthings*; and thefe are a legal tender in all fums below fix-pence, which now is our fmalleft current filver coin.

The ufe of copper coins fhould be ftrictly confined within the above limit; and therein they are very convenient: But thefe bafe coins fhould never be thruft upon the public in too great abundance; or be made to pafs for more than the value of the copper, and the neceffary expence of workmanfhip; otherwife, they will be counter-

F   feited

feited, notwithſtanding any laws to the contrary. And to leſſen the call for copper
coins, it were to be wiſhed that we had in
common currency, either ſilver three-pences,
or ſilver groats, and two-pences.

XI. *Money finds its own value, according to
the whole quantity of it in circulation.*

40. The quantities of all commodities
are proportioned, as near as may be, according to the demand or vent for them ; and
their ultimate prices include the prime coſt,
and the profits taken by the ſeveral dealers,
thro' whoſe hands they paſs : If the quantity of any commodity exceeds, or falls ſhort
of that proportion, its price will fall or riſe
accordingly ; and ſometimes, a change of
faſhion, or humour, may reduce the price
of a particular commodity, almoſt to nothing. The prices of things in general are
proportioned ſufficiently near, according to
the above rule ; or, according to their prime
coſt to the manufacturer, and the progreſs
they make from him to the conſumer. But
ſome things, as above obſerved, are ſubject
to be reduced by caprice much below this
ſtandard ; whilſt others are raiſed much
above it, by the arts and avarice of mo-
nopolizers. And although the ſilver and
gold

gold mines, are in few hands; yet, perhaps, there is nothing whofe value is fo little in the power of men to regulate, or that keeps fo even a pace with the quantity fent to the great market of the world, as bullion. For,

Money, exchanging univerfally for all commodities, the demand for it is without any limits; it is every where coveted, and never out of fafhion : And therefore, on the one fide, the whole quantity of money, cannot exceed the whole demand; and on the other fide, the whole demand muft not exceed, or it muft reft fatisfied with, the whole quantity. For money, is not like food, cloaths, and other things, that muft be proportioned to our bodies.

Therefore, as foon as money becomes properly diffufed throughout any community; the value of the fum total of it in circulation, will be equal to the whole quantity of commodities in traffic, in that country : For fo much money and goods as lie dormant, or are out of currency and traffic, fall not within the prefent confideration *. And fo far as gold and filver, make

the

---

* There is always a great part of the property of mankind, lying dormant, or out of traffic : But as things are continually fhifting, and thofe commodities, and thofe fums of money, which are out of trade to-day, may be in trade

the money of the world; fo far, the whole
quantity of thefe metals in circulation, may
be faid to be equal in value to all the commodities of the world, exchangeable by
them : And as the total of the one, is to
the total of the other; fo will any given
part of the one, be to a like part or proportion of the other.

. And hence, the value of a given quantity or fum of money, in any country, will
be lefs or more, according as the fum total,
or the whole quantity of money in currency, is greater or lefs, in proportion to
the whole of the commodities of that country, exchangeable for money : Or, *the va-*
lue of a given fum of money will be always,
pretty exactly, in a reciprocal proportion to
the fum total, or the whole quantity in cir-
culation; that is, the more money there is
in currency, the lefs will be the value of a
given fum in proportion to other things;
and *vice versâ.* Hence again, it naturally
follows, that, *if,* in any country, *the whole*
quantity of money in circulation, be either in-
creafed, or diminifhed; *the value of a given*
fum will be accordingly leffened or increafed *;
and

to-morrow; the prices of things always fundamentally depend upon the above rule ; that is, on the proportion of the
total of things to the total of money.
* Thus, if in any country, a given fum *A* be the hundredth part of the total money of that country : If that
fum

*and that in proportion, as the said sum be-
comes thereby, a lesser or a greater part, of
the whole stock in currency.*

The above * proposition, is a very fundamental one as to the property of money;
and the doctrine it contains is undoubtedly
proved, as far as the nature of the thing
will admit of, by universal experience : Nor
is there room for any doubt to remain,
when it is considered that money, by its
very institution, is an exchange for all commodities; and applicable, as money, to no
other purpose whatsoever. Money being
universally diffused, no one hath the power
to command the market, or to settle the
prices of things; and every one being de-
sirous to have his share of things, according to his income; all the money, in the
long run, will be brought into the great
market of the world ; and its value, or the
prices of things, will naturally be adjusted,
notwithstanding any efforts to the contrary,
according to the proportions above explained.

F 3   By

sum total be doubled, the value of the sum *A* will be there
by reduced to one half, as being now but a two hundredth
part of the whole ; and had the sum total been reduced to
a half, the value of *A* would have been doubled.

* From this proposition, all the following ones in this
chapter, naturally flow as corollaries ; but on the account of
their importance, they are treated and illustrated severally

By way of farther illuftration of this
fubject: Let us fuppofe that in a certain diftrict, there is ordinarily confumed a thoufand bufhels of corn a week ; and that,
(after their money is duly proportioned for
the purchafing of all other neceffaries, according to the ways of living of the inhabitants,) the weekly allotment for the purchafe of corn, is a thoufand ounces of money : The price of a bufhel of corn, at an
average of the feveral markets within this
diftrict, will be an ounce of money. Let
us fuppofe again, that within the faid diftrict, the ordinary * confumption of a labouring man, or rather of a poor family,
is about the value of a bufhel of corn a
week ; part of which is expended in bread,
part in other food, and the remainder is
referved for the purchafe of cloaths, fuel,
for the payment of rent, &c. Here then,
the price of labour will be at the rate of
about an ounce of money *per* week ; the
loweft kind of labourers having a little lefs,
and the common artificers a little more,
than

* The way of living of the lower clafs of people, will
be naturally beft and moft comfortable, in the happy re-
gions of liberty ; where property is duly diffufed ; where
there is a gradual and an eafy tranfition from rank to rank ;
without that ghaftly and fearful void between peers and
peafants, betwixt tyrants and flaves, which is ever the baneful fruit of arbitrary governments.   3

than in the faid proportion. And hence, labour becomes naturally fettled, in a certain proportion to the whole ftock of money in circulation; and this price again becomes, as hath been before obferved, a natural ftandard of the values or prices of moft commodities.

XII. *Laws cannot regulate or alter the value of money.*

41. Silver being made money, and thereby becoming, as it were, a commodity univerfally coveted; wherein every one deals, and to which every one hath a right, according to his refpective fhare of property: No fet of men have it in their power to fettle, alter, or in any wife regulate the value of money; nor can laws do any thing in the cafe, otherwife than as by their influence, they may increafe or diminifh, the whole quantity in circulation; and fo affect the value of a given fum, or the prices of things.

The prices of particular commodities are every day fubject to change, from natural caufes; and the fame may be brought about, by artificial means. But to alter the value of money, would be to alter uniformly and univerfally, the prices of all commodities;

a

a thing manifeftly out of the reach of laws, and no other way to be accomplifhed, than by altering the proportion between the fum total of the one, and the fum total of the other ; and this, perhaps, is continually done, though gradually and infenfibly, by the common courfe of things.

It is the bufinefs of laws to eftablifh rules for coining ; that is, to fix a ftandard, both as to weight and finenefs, for coins having certain denominations ; and a ftandard being fixed, it would be difficult to fhew, why it fhould be afterwards deviated from. For, do what you can ; coins, as foon as they are out of the mint, are quite free throughout their whole progrefs, to find their own value, according to the quantity of pure metal they contain ; that is, to purchafe as much of any thing, as the market-price will allow. And it feems quite a paralogifm to fay, which yet I have often heard faid, that in any country, money is either too cheap or too dear ; or, that its value is in any wife fubject to legal reftraints or regulations, otherwife than as fuch regulations might affect the quantity of the whole ftock in currency.

Value

Value of bullion not according to the prime
coſt at the mines.

42. The value of bullion doth not, like moſt other things, keep pace with the prime coſt, at the mines. If the mines continue working, ſo that the quantity of bullion is increaſed beyond the confumption; altho' the expence to the proprietor of the mine continues the ſame, or even be increaſed; yet, if the additional quantity of bullion be thrown as money into circulation, and is not hoarded, or worked up into plate, *&c.* the value of a given part of this bullion will be diminiſhed; and that in proportion, as it is now a leſs part of the whole, than it was of the old ſtock in circulation. The owner of the mine, muſt either take leſs profit, or proportion his works more ade-quately to the confumption of his products.

An increaſe of any commodity beyond the confumption, will, after the ſame man-ner, depreciate the value of a given part; but perhaps in no caſe ſo uniformly, as in that of bullion or money.

As the profits from the *American* mines, have, more than probably, been continu-ally decreaſing, ever ſince the time of their firſt diſcovery; it may be wondered, that
they

they have held out fo long to yield profit
fufficient to tempt the owners to work them.
This is to be accounted for, by fuppofing,
what is very natural to fuppofe, that at firft,
the profits of thefe mines, were exorbitantly great : Suppofe that the firft cargo of
bullion, brought from thence into *Europe*,
yielded a profit of 100 to 1 : If this cargo
was fufficient to double the quantity of bullion before in *Europe*, the profits of the
next would be reduced to one half, or as
50 to 1 ; and fo on, the value of a given
part would be decreafed, as the fum total
was increafed.

But as the navigation to the *Eaft-Indies*,
was difcovered much about the fame time,
and a vent was found there for a confiderable quantity of bullion ; this hath
prevented its value from decreafing, in
the proportion that the quantity brought
into *Europe* hath increafed ; and fufficient
profits may yet arife from thofe mines,
for a confiderable time to come. But, although we fhould fuppofe thofe mines to
be inexhauftible ; yet, if no new vent be
found for their products, they muft in time
be left to reft ; that is, as foon as they ceafe
to yield a profit.

XIII.

XIII. *Money alters its value by flow degrees.*

43. It is very manifeſt, that many commodities are ſubject to conſiderable variations in their prices, from natural cauſes;
as dearth, plenty, *&c.* and the prices of
others, may be enhanced or debaſed by artificial methods; by taxing them, or by a
change of faſhion, *&c.* But money being
univerſally coveted, and its vent in no wiſe
depending upon faſhion; its value, in reſpect of other things, will be, as before obſerved, in proportion to the whole quantities of the one and the other in the market; that is, in a reciprocal proportion to
the whole quantity of money in circulation.
If one commodity be cried down, another
will ariſe in its ſtead; and people will, according to their means, part with their money for ſuch things, and in ſuch proportion
too, as they like beſt, notwithſtanding any
laws to the contrary. Buyers and ſellers
muſt be left free to make their own bargains; and there are natural cauſes that regulate the market.

But money is leſs ſubject to a ſudden riſe
or fall of its value, than other commodities, and is therefore ſo far the ſafeſt trea-
ſure

fure for hoarding ; becaufe its value is greatly affected by fettled eftablifhments of revenues, rents, ftipends, &c. and it muft have
time alfo to penetrate throughout the whole
community. Yet neverthelefs, an increafe
or decreafe of money will operate as furely,
though by flower and more infenfible degrees, as an increafe or decreafe of any commodity.

Why the effect of an increafe of money, is
not more fenfibly felt.

44. As there hath been a great quantity
of bullion annually imported from *America*,
befides what is furnifhed by the *European*
mines ; it may be reafonably concluded, that
the quantity of money in *Europe*, hath been
increafing for many years ; and the prefent
prices of things in general, compared with
what they bore a good while ago, very
manifeftly fhews that it hath increafed. But
if we take a fhort fpace, as a year or two,
the effects of the increafe of money in that
time, are not ufually perceptible ; becaufe
the fuperadded quantity, though in its felf
a large fum, may yet bear but a fmall proportion to the whole ftock, real or imaginary, in circulation ; and it may be in a manner diffipated, before it hath reached to all

forts

forts of commodities. Yet, if there be no obstructions, the effects of an increase or decrease of money, will in time reach to the remotest parts; though, by reason of their flowness or smallness, those effects may not be sensible.

The natural and frequent alterations in the prices of many commodities, arising from their greater plenty or scarcity, in proportion to the demand for them; take off our attention from the share that belongs to money, and render the effects of an increase or decrease of its quantity, the less conspicuous. But yet these effects, in the long run, will not be the less certain: And we may safely repeat here, what hath been before advanced, *viz.*

Any given sum or quantity of money, will have its value in a certain proportion, as it is a part of the whole stock or quantity in currency; and any increase or diminution of the whole, will in proportion, lessen or increase the value of any given sum.

Why the prices of commodities, have not rose in proportion to the increase of money.

45. It is next to impossible to ascertain, to any exactness, the proportion between what is the present cash of *Europe,* and
what

what it was two or three centuries ago; for one of the *Indies*, drains away a great part of the fuperfluous bullion of the other. Nor will the price of any particular commodity, or of even labour it felf, which is perhaps the beft ftandard of all, enable us to make a true eftimate. For, the improvements of arts, leffen the values or prices of particular commodities; and the improvements of hufbandry, in particular, leffen the prices of corn and cattle; and thence again, the price of labour will be leffened.

From all thefe confiderations, it is natural to fuppofe that the quantities of goods in *Europe*, have increafed, fince the difcovery of the *Indies*, far beyond the people; and therefore, the value of any given commodity hath leffened, in proportion as the fum total or whole ftock of commodities hath been increafed. And if all the above circumftances could be accurately ballanced; I make no doubt but it would be found, that the prices of things are agreeable to the rule before laid down; that is, the *value* of any particular commodity, will bear nearly the fame proportion to the fum total of commodities, difpofed of within a given term; as the faid *value* bears to the fum total of money, circulating within that term.

The

The totals on both fides, being always equal, or nearly equal, in value; fo that either can purchafe the other.

But, without confidering the increafe of commodities; there may be another caufe of preventing the value of money from decreafing, in the fame proportion that the quantity of bullion brought to *Europe* is increafed. If the annual confumption of bullion in *Europe*, both by the *Eaft-India* trade, and by the converfion of it into plate, be equal to what the *American* mines annually fupply; the value of money taken abftractedly, or without referring it to commodities, will remain invariable : But if the faid confumption be lefs, or more, than the faid produce of the mines; the whole quantity of money will be accordingly increafed, or diminifhed; and the value of a given part or fum, will be leffened, or increafed, in that proportion.

It is the real quantity of coins, or of their fubftitutes, that affects the value of money. And this, together with the improvements of arts and increafe of commodities; is the reafon, why things in general have not raifed in their prices, in proportion to the fuppofed increafe of bullion in *Europe*, during the laft 200 years.

XIV.

XIV. *A nation having no foreign commerce, will not stand in need of any specific quantity of money.*

46. In a country having no foreign commerce, any quantity of money will, in a manner, be sufficient for all purposes ; and any increase or diminution of the original stock, if it be but gradual and flow, will scarce be attended with any consequences of moment. This, although to many it may seem a paradox, yet clearly follows from what hath been already shewed. But as a farther illustration of this subject:

Let us suppose that many ages ago, a certain nation consisted of half a million of people, and that they had in the whole a million of pounds sterling ; and that afterwards the mines or the mint were no farther worked, than to keep the money exactly to the same or the original quantity of a million. We may suppose also, that a regular government, and all the necessary arts, were established amongst them ; and likewise that all the money was distributed betwixt them, in due proportion according to their several ranks ; so that the hire of a labourer, we will suppose, was ten-pence

a

a day. By degrees, they increase in number one tenth; and with the people, all sorts of commodities, naturally increase in proportion: But the whole quantity of money remaining the same, its value increased also one tenth; and nine-pence now going as far as ten-pence would before, the wages of a day-labourer is reduced one penny: But this he doth not feel the want of; and he hath as much plenty of all sorts of necessaries now, as he had formerly.

In process of time, and that before they had any foreign commerce, the people are increased to five millions; and the price of labour, which at first was ten-pence, is now reduced to a penny a day. All this while, there were no complaints of the want of money, though every one's share came to but a tenth part of what his ancestors possessed. On the contrary, by the improvements of the arts they had set out with, and the inventions of many new ones; all ranks of people lived more comfortably, with more ease and affluence than their fore-fathers had done.

By these improvements of the arts, the whole stock of commodities was increased beyond the increase of the people; and each particular commodity bore less than

a tenth part of its antient price : More people in proportion could be fpared from labour, for particular fervices and profeffions;
for in many of the arts, one man could per-
form now, more than two men could formerly. With the increafe of the people,
the taxes on each individual grew naturally
lighter ; and yet the government grew daily
more powerful and fplendid : Altho' rents
and all other things, funk in their nominal
values ; yet a greater affluence and fplendor
of living, was every where to be feen.   So
true it is, that numbers of induftrious people, and not money, is what enriches a
country.

   Had the money increafed with the people, that would have made no manner of
difference in the values of things with refpect to one another ; nor would it have
been very material, if the orignal ftock of
money had decreafed upon their hands; the
only difference which that would have created, would have been in the nominal prices
of things with refpect to money.   Had the
money increafed fafter than the people, fuppofe 24 times ; the price of labour would
have become then 20 fhillings a day, and
yet the workman would have been no ways
benefited by that greatnefs of wages.

                                   The

The cafe above fuppofed of the quantity
of money remaining invariable, whilft the
people increafed, is the very fame in effect,
as if we had fuppofed the number of people to have continued the fame, whilft the
original ftock of money had continually decreafed.

XV. *Any fudden fluctation of money, would
be pernicious.*

47. Money as fuch, though very ufeful
and neceffary in all forts of traffic, yet fcarce
falls within the idea of riches *. Money
in its very inftitution, is profeffedly of no
ufe, but to meafure the value of, and as an
exchange for, things that are ufeful : It is
fo much coveted, not for its own fake, but
for what it will bring ; and it is very manifeft, that in a regular and well-eftablifhed
community, a greater or lefs ftock of money doth fcarce at all affect its wealth and
profperity †. The greateft effect of money
is in its fluctuation, and this if it be fudden
will be generally pernicious in its confequences.

G 2 If

* Money is here confidered in the abftract ; but as it is
reducible into bullion, plate, &c. in that fenfe it is wealth
like other commodities.
† This hath been fhewed in the preceding, as to a nation hav'ng no foreign commerce ; how far fuch a commerce alters the cafe, will be confidered a little farther on.

If money be a flowing in, some branches
of trade will be enlivened, and in reality
great numbers of individuals will grow richer;
as what they pay in taxes, rents, and for
* natural products, will be less or of less
value than before; till you come to the
lowest class, who, though their wages are
raised, will yet find little or no advantage
by this torrent of money. On the other
hand, the government will grow weaker,
the nobility, and in general all who live
upon estates and established stipends, will
become poorer; till by an increase of taxes,
advancement of rents, &c. things can be
re-established. But before this can be accomplished, many and great alterations will
naturally happen : The government being
thus weakened and distressed, disorders will
inevitably arise ; as peace and good order
cannot be preserved, unless the strength of
the government bears a due proportion to
that of the governed : The nobility must
change their fashion of life, and abate of
their antient splendor ; new debts will be
contracted, increased, lands mortgaged ; and
before

* It will be some time before this supposed additional
money can penetrate through all the branches of trade, and
whilst some traders have exorbitant gains, others will grow
poorer, because of their additional expence in many articles;
however by degrees all dealers will help themselves, and
grow rich at the expence of those who are mere consumers.

before the antient owners have a right underſtanding of the cauſe of their diſtreſſes,
many muſt part with their eſtates, and give
place to new comers.

And this is a natural conſequence of a
ſudden flux of money; * the enriching of
one part of the community, at the expence
of the other; a change of manners amongſt
all ranks, ſome perhaps for the better, and
ſome for the worſe; until, this tide having
ſpent itſelf, things are again reſettled, tho'
perhaps in quite a new form.

On the other hand, if the tide of money
is a running out; during this ebb, trade
will ſtagnate, ſome merchants and ſhop-
keepers will break, ſome manufactures will
be laid aſide, many hands will be unem-
ployed, and murmurs and complaints will
be heard among all ſorts of people concerned in trade. Theſe diſtreſſes will continue,
till by an abatement of taxes, lowering of
rents, of wages, of ſtipends, &c. a due
equilibrium among the different ranks of
people is again reſtored; and then, altho'

* How far this may have been the caſe of ſome particular
country, I do not here conſider. But I think it is manifeſt
enough, that an overflow of money in one place, may be
the cauſe of poverty and diſtreſſes in another; and that a
government may be declining, whilſt duties and cuſtoms are
increaſing.

a great part of the money is gone, riches, plenty, and good order, will again abound.

Thus it is manifeſt, that a ſudden fluctuation of money, would be pernicious whilſt it laſted, and for ſome time afterwards * ; and that whether the tide be flowing in or going out. But whilſt it glides and circulates ſmoothly and freely, in its natural courſe and channels, money is not only a harmleſs but a beneficial thing ; it cheriſhes and invigorates the whole community, and this equally, whether the ſtream be large or ſlender.

XVI. *Ballance of trade, what.*

48. The ultimate ballance of trade is reckoned in money ; and it is by this ſcale that the profits of trade are uſually computed. But as money in it ſelf is of no farther uſe, but merely as a kind of inſtrument for the circulation of products or commodities ; a very beneficial commerce may be carried on between different nations, without any of them having any money to receive at the cloſe of their accounts. Not only the mariners navigating the ſhips, but alſo

---

* The effects of the imaginary increaſe of money in the year 1720, and of the real increaſe of factitious money at different periods ſince, do greatly illuſtrate and corroborate what hath been here advanced.

alſo the whole train of artificers employed
in the various branches of manufaures,
bred and nouriſhed by ſuch a commerce,
innumerable brokers, &c. gain all of them
a comfortable ſubſiſtence : Each country is
accommodated, with what it wanted of the
produs of the other ; and the * merchants
on all ſides increaſe in wealth, though at
laſt their accounts are even as to money, or
yet though one pays a ballance in money
to the other.

If bullion be the ſole or chief end of
commerce; why are ſhips ſent to any other
ports, beſides *Cadiz* and *Liſbon ?* Silver and
gold are in a manner, the peculiar commodities of *Spain* and *Portugal*; and in the
uſual phraſe, theſe nations muſt pay a ballance upon their trade to all the world.
And yet they, as well as the reſt of the
world, are gainers by trade; they obtain
various neceſſaries and conveniences, which
their bullion could not have procured them,
whilſt they kept it at home; and ſo long
as they keep working the mines, ſo long
probably they will ſtand in more need of

G 4   the

---

* That is, each merchant is a gainer, if his returns, after
paying all his expences of the voyage, are worth at home
more, or will purchaſe again a greater quantity of goods
than he had exported : This overplus is the merchant's profit, without which he would no longer trade.

the aid of foreign commerce, than other
nations.

A ballance paid in money, doth not
neceffarily infer a lofs by trade: Suppofe
that laft year, *Great Britain* paid a ballance upon the whole of its foreign trade,
of a hundred thoufand pounds in fpecie;
but that the national ftock of neceffaries, in
naval ftores of various forts, &c. were increafed to double that value: By the ufual
reckoning, we muft have loft the laft year,
an 100,000 *l.* by our trade; but by mine,
we were gainers by it to the net value of
that whole fum. But had the above fuppofed additional ftock of foreign commodities, been in wines, brandies, fine linnens,
toys, or even jewels, &c. which were to be
all confumed at home, I fhould readily have
joined in the common eftimation, of our
having been lofers by our trade. Gold and
filver are valuable commodities, becaufe they
are neither perifhable, nor over bulky; and
becaufe the monies of the world are made of
thefe metals, they retain a more even and
permanent value, and are more univerfally
coveted than other things. But the *Spa-
niards* are an inftance, that a nation may be
injured, weakened and impoverifhed, by an
over-ftock of thefe metals.

How-

However, any nation having gained upon the whole of its commerce a ballance in bullion, may be truly faid to be a gainer for that time of fo much as that bullion amounts to; and if it can keep that bullion as a dead ftock, either by turning it into plate or by any other method, fo as to prevent its getting into trade as money; it may continue to go on increafing in more bullion, which in this cafe will be a real increafe of wealth. For as bullion hath little or no workmanfhip beftowed upon it, and is every where after it hath once got from the miner's hands, a kind of dead ftock, applied to no ufe like other commodities; a nation that pays ultimately upon its trade a ballance in bullion, is a lofer of fo much of its dead ftock; and a lofer alfo, if its exports maintained fewer of its own inhabitants, than its imports did of thofe of foreign nations. Let an increafed ftock of bullion get out again into trade, and it will foon turn the ballance the other way.

XVII. *The quantity of money every where, will naturally find a certain level or proportion.*

49. It is a received opinion, at leaft with many people, that a certain fpecific

3

cific

cific quantity of money, is neceſſary for the carrying on of foreign commerce; and that any nation not abounding in money, will trade to a great diſadvantage with the reſt of the world : Were this the caſe, thoſe nations who have moſt money, ſhould reap moſt advantage by trade; and *Spain* and *Portugal* ought to carry the prize from all the world.   But if this matter be examined, ever ſo ſlightly, it will appear in a different light; and it will appear alſo, that no trading nation can be long in want of money, or be able to keep above a certain quantity of circulating caſh, in proportion to its trade. What is hoarded and kept out of the market, either in caſh, bullion, plate or furniture of any ſort, is out of the preſent queſtion.

Suppoſe that the preſent ſtock of circulating caſh in *England*, was at once reduced to one half, by each perſon's loſing a moiety of his own ſhare.   This would ſtrike a great conſternation in all, and be matter of real calamity to many; as the prices of things would not at once abate, in proportion to this great loſs of money.   But thoſe diſtreſſes would not laſt long : The prices of all commodities, and of labour, would fall by degrees; this cheapneſs would give
them

them a quicker vent in all foreign markets, and all forts of manufactures would be carried on here brifker than ever; whilft at the fame time, and for the fame caufe, the confumption of foreign commodities with us would be greatly diminifhed. By the cheapnefs of labour, *England* becoming the beft market for bullion; that is, bullion fetching more labour and commodities here than in other countries, it would naturally be fent hither preferable to other things; and bullion would not ceafe flowing in upon us, till it became as cheap, that is, in as great plenty here, in proportion to our traffic, as in other places.

This fuppofed fudden lofs of money would at firft, as hath been before illuftrated, create many diforders: By the fudden change it would caufe in the proportion of property, a damp would be thrown upon manufactures, until the price of labour could be duly reduced; and the nation would be under a great difadvantage, in the purchafing of foreign commodities for ready cafh. But thefe difadvantages would not laft long; and whilft things were advancing towards their former ftate, it is probable that people in general, efpecially the lower clafs, who are the moft numerous, would

would abound more in affluence than at any
other period. Labour would be more valuable here, in proportion to commodities ;
becaufe of the great demand for thofe commodities, in thofe countries where money
was cheaper, and labour dearer ; until at
length the equilibrium of money was again
reftored. Had we fuppofed the lofs of money to have been lefs, as only, for inftance,
the tenth part; the confequences thereupon,
though lefs perceptible, would have been,
upon the whole, the fame in a proportionable degree.

Let us fuppofe our former ftock of money to be now completely reftored to us,
and it would not be long before it returned
again : If we think to increafe this ftock
much farther, we fhall be difappointed ;
the caufes that brought it to a certain level,
will prevent its rifing much above that
level. Where money is grown into great
plenty, whatever be the caufes of that over-
plenty ; labour, and all forts of manufactures will grow dear, too dear for foreign
markets : And at the fame time that the
exportation of home - commodities is decreafing, that of bullion for foreign goods
will be increafing ; till at length the tide
of the over-plenty of money hath fpent its
                                              felf;

felf; leaving behind it perhaps, too much the marks of profufion, and diforders of various kinds.

In order to illuftrate this fubject, I have fuppofed cafes that are not likely to happen; the ftate of things, altho' ever fluctuating, yet change by flow degrees. Riches are comparative things; and one nation's growing or declining in wealth, is to be reckoned either with refpect to its former ftate, or the prefent ftate of its neighbours. But the queftion before us being folely about money, which ever way that is turned, it feems to me evident, that commerce will fettle the due proportion of money every where; I mean the proportion in refpect to the whole wealth and traffic of any country, and not the proportion between one country and another; for this laft will be ever different and ever variable. Every one fees that an increafe of his own cafh would be an advantage to him, and hence money is univerfally coveted; but no one fees or confiders, that his own peculiar advantage would ceafe, if every body's cafh was increafed in the fame proportion with his own. Another hath in his eye fome beneficial trade, which he could enter into if

he

he had but money * : It is none of his bu-
fineſs to conſider, that the trade of the
world is limited ; that his entering into it,
would not extend trade in general. It is
the want of vent, and not the want of money, that limits trade ; and ſometimes alſo
the want of able and ſkilful workmen re-
moves trade from one province or kingdom
into another.

All that hath been here advanced, is well illuſtrated and corroborated, by the courſe that
manufaɛturies have taken in our own country.   They have been firſt erecɛted in parts
that had but little money in common currency; that is, in places where labour, proviſions, and all the neceſſaries of life were
cheap : By degrees they enriched thoſe provinces, till at length proviſions of all ſorts,
and conſequently labour, became very dear;
too dear to ſuſtain, or to be ſuſtained by
thoſe manufaɛturies any longer.   This naturally carried them to other places, where
money

* The common trite ſaying, " that if a merchant had a
" a larger ſtock, he could afford to ſell cheaper," anſwers it
ſelf: If his ſtock is but ſmall, he ſhould himſelf conſume
leſs.   If a rich galleon was to be divided among a certain
number of our merchants, this would enable them indeed
to buy dearer and to ſell cheaper ; but this would be detrimental both to their cotemporaries and ſucceſſors, and I
think, in the long run, to their country in general.   For ſo
far as it went, it would enhance the price of commodities at
home, and leſſen their vent at foreign markets.

money was in lefs plenty : And this will
ever be the cafe, unlefs part of the increafed ftock of money is kept out of the
common circulation, and is either hoarded
or directed into fome new channel; without this, not only trade will move to different provinces of the fame country, but
it will move alfo into different countries.

XVIII. *Any artificial methods of increafing*
tale-money, pernicious.

50. Any artificial methods of increafing
the quantity of tale-money in circulation,
beyond its natural bounds, will be attended
with pernicious confequences; and this effect is perhaps not the leaft evil of our great
national debt. As the values of all things
are meafured by money, it is, I think, by
this time fufficiently manifeft, that their
prices will be in a certain proportion to the
whole quantity of cafh in circulation. If
this quantity be greater in proportion to the
trade of the nation, than in foreign countries; things manufactured at home will become too dear for foreign markets, as is the
cafe of *Spain* and *Portugal.* As we have
no mines, trade will keep, as before obferved, real money to a proper level; but
yet this level may be exceeded by artificial
                                        fub-

substitutes, as paper-bills, having no bullion
locked up in their stead, and light coins
having less value than what they pass for;
and by both these methods the nation is injured : By making all things dearer at home,
the public is not only defrauded of so much
bullion as these substitutes amount to; that
is, to the whole amount of the paper above
the bullion locked up in its stead; but it also
suffers by the loss of the whole deficiency
upon the light coins.

Although this subject hath been in effect
illustrated before, yet is it of that importance as to deserve to be farther exemplified.
Let us suppose that one tenth of the whole
stock of circulating cash in this country,
and 'tis not material to our argument what
the specific sum amounts to, is some way
lost or destroyed: If no artificial substitutes
be made to intervene; it has been before
shewed, that trade will gradually restore this
supposed loss of bullion; as, till this be
accomplished, bullion will be dearer or fetch
more commodities here, than in other countries.

On the other hand, supposing the sum
total of money, real and fictitious, now annually circulating in this country, to be 100
millions; 20 millions of which is in cash,
and

and the reft in paper credit both public
and private: If this paper credit be increafed,
by the creating of more bills, fuppofe to
the amount of ten millions; one of the following will neceffarily be the confequence:
Either all our commodities will rife ten
per cent. in their nominal value, which will
render them too dear for foreign markets;
or, this addition of paper bills will drain
away ten millions of our cafh, and fo impoverifh us in reality to that whole amount;
or, the effect moft likely will be, partly the
one, and partly the other; but which ever
it is, the nation will be equally endamaged.
May this be ever a caution to ftatefmen,
how they liften to projects that muft clog
our trade, banifh our coin, and in the end
bring on a general bankruptcy.

Let us fuppofe again, that the fame quantity of tale or nominal money continues,
but that the real fubftance of the current
coin is diminifhed one tenth. So long as
the people pay no regard to this diminution,
the prices of things will continue the fame
as before, and the nation will be a lofer of
this tenth part of its treafure. For, if the
currency of the light coins had been ftopped; or, which is the fame thing, if they
bad been reftrained from paffing otherwife

H   than

than by weight; trade would have furnifhed the fame quantity of tale in heavy
money, as there is now of light; as it is
manifeft that in both cafes, the nominal
prices of things would be the fame; and
every one would receive for the fame fervice or commodity, the fame number of
heavy coins in the one cafe, as he would of
light coins in the other.   Foreign exchange
may make fome difference here ; but as the
ballance of foreign trade is but fmall in comparifon of fixed eftablifhments at home, the
difference upon that account will not be very
confiderable, till things come towards an
extremity.

What hath been faid of the national lofs
by the paffing of light coins, will hold the
very fame, if bills be paffed to a greater value
than there is bullion in their ftead.   All
private fecurities alfo are productive of equal
evils, and frequently of more.   To clofe
this fubject, I would obferve here one effential difference there is between bills and
light coins.   Every one hath a right to call
upon the iffuer of a bill, to make it good in
ftandard or lawful money.   But he that
hath light coins in his poffeffion, is liable
to bear the whole lofs that there may be
upon them; he took them in full confideration

tion of a given fum, and if they prove deficient, he hath no body to blame but himfelf;
and he merits the lefs compaffion, as by
his unwarinefs he was a fharer in, and a
promoter of, a public evil.

Hoarding the precious metals, beneficial.

51. Gold and filver, for many reafons,
are the fitteft materials hitherto known for
hoarding: They are durable; convertible
without damage into any form; of great value in proportion to their bulk; and being
the money of the world, they are the rea-
dieft exchange for all things, and what moft
readily and furely command all kinds of
fervices. In the days of profperity therefore, it would be prudent to lay up a kind
of dead ftock of the precious metals, againft
any emergencies that might happen. This
ftock muft be kept out from the circulating cafh; for an increafe there, would not
anfwer the end; and indeed an overflow of
money in circulation, would fpend it felf,
by draining up the fources that produced
it. But people in general will not hoard up
cafh; all like to difplay their wealth, and
to lay out their fuperfluities in fome coftly
things. There feems then no method fo
effectual for the fecuring of a dead ftock of

trea-

treafure, in any country, as the encourag-
ing the ufe of plate; by making it fafhion-
able, preferable to more brittle or more perifhable * commodities. Plate would be a
national refource in cafe of emergency, and
not the lefs fo, becaufe the precious metals
had not as yet received the fhape of coins.
But this dead ftock, whilft it remained fuch,
would not be without its ufe; real wealth
is ever accompanied with credit, and the influence of credit is frequently of the greateft
moment. He that is ready armed, is lefs
liable to be affailed; and filver and gold are
keen and deftructive weapons.

XIX. *Of Banks.*

52. The feveral banks now fubfifting in
Europe, are of a modern date; but it is
not my intention here to meddle either with
their hiftories or particular conftitutions. In
great trading cities, a public bank that
iffued no bills without an equivalent in real
treafure, whether in cafh or bullion it matters

---

* I have fpoke before in favour of the arts, and I would
not here be underftood to mean, that any of thofe whereby
fome of our own people gain a livelihood, fhould be dif-
couraged; nor yet that thofe of narrow circumftances, fhould
aim at having plate: But thofe of affluent fortunes might
fave themfelves the expence of many fuperfluities, without
affecting labour with us; and thefe favings laid out in plate
would be of more benefit to their country, and to their own
pofterity.

ters not much, muſt needs, I think, be very
convenient; as therein, merchants and others
may ſafely depoſite large ſums, and thence
again draw their money out at ſuch times,
and in ſuch ſmall parcels, as may ſuit with
their ſeveral occaſions. Such a bank may
be alſo of ſome ſupport to national credit, as
the great ſums known to be there locked
up, would be ready upon an emergency.
Bills of undoubted credit, are of great conveniency in large payments, and beſides, ſave
the wear of coin. But their extent ſhould
be reſtrained within due bounds: Should
they increaſe much beyond the real ſtock
of bullion that ought to be in their ſtead,
they would prove miſchievous two ways;
by increaſing in effect the quantity of circulating caſh beyond its natural level ; and
by endangering, in a cloudy day, their own
credit. But the profits to be made by lend-
ing, as I may ſay, of credit, are tempta-
tions too ſtrong to be reſiſted; and it may
be queſtioned, if any of the banks now
ſubſiſting, keep exactly within the above
rule, tho' ſome of them are formed upon
the very model here laid down.

*Banks inftituted to prevent the abufes from
    bad coins, and from adulterations in the
    ftandards of monies.*

53. The oldeft bank now in *Europe*, I
think, is that of *Venice*; and the chief, if
not all, of the reft, were inftituted in the
laft century, and much upon the fame model.   The bank of *Amfterdam* was eftablifhed in 1607; that of *Hamburgh* in 1619,
and that of *Nuremburgh* in 1621 *.

It appears, that the main if not the fole defign of erecting thefe banks, was for the fixing a kind of an indelible ftandard of money;
and thereby, to fecure merchants and others
from loffes by bad coins, whether bafe or
light; and from the dire effects of adulterating the ftandards of monies, either at
home, or by the neighbouring ftates. Thefe
banks have anfwered admirably well the
ends of their inftitution; and it were to be
wifhed, that thofe ends had been more regarded in the eftablifhment of our own.
At the times of eftablifhing the above banks,
certain known coins of given weights and
finenefs, then current at certain rates in the
                                                    refpective

* See more upon this head, in the *Univerfal Merchant*,
a work containing fome judicious obfervations concerning
trade.

refpective places, were fixed upon as·a perpetual ftandard, which from thenceforward
were called BANK MONEY. As the cur- *Bank mo-*
rent coins became afterwards diminifhed, *ney, what.*
either by legal adulterations at the mints, or
by wear, or otherwife, a diftinction was
made between current and bank money,
called AGGIO; and according to the real *Aggio,*
difference between thefe two forts of mo- *what.*
ney, the *aggio* amounted to more or lefs
per cent. Thefe wife eftablifhments contri-
buted greatly, towards ftopping thofe baneful
meafures of adulterating the ftandards of money, that had been fo frequently and fo generally practifed, in the dark preceding ages.
The genius of trade breathes and requires
a certain degree of fecurity and freedom;
and banks, fuch as we have been fpeaking
of, can hardly ever take place under arbitrary governments.

Complaints of the want of money, whence.

54. The doctrine that we have been inculcating is fo contrary to the common notions, that a want of money is a common
cry. All the fcramble is for money; few
think they have enough, and many complain. This probably will be ever the cafe,
nor would fetting the mint to work cure

the

the evil; and perhaps there is no where
more want, than where there is moſt money.
The beggar hath no property, nothing to
exchange for money; and if he will not
work, none would come to his ſhare, if the
common ſtock was ever ſo much increaſed;
a greater plenty of money would be ſo far
from being advantageous to him, that he
would run the greater riſk of ſtarving, as
bread and proviſions of all ſorts would
then be ſo much the dearer.   The farmer
complains, and thinks that if there was
more money in the country, his corn and
cattle would fetch a better price : They
would fetch more money, but not more of
any thing elſe that he wants; and he would
not be at all bettered by this higher price,
unleſs ſo far as a ſudden increaſe of money might eaſe him in his rent, by leſſening the intrinſic value of the ſpecific ſum
which he had agreed to pay.   The ſame
may be ſaid to the merchant, ſhop-keeper,
&c. while all commodities keep the ſame
proportion of value in reſpect of one another,
no one reaps any advantage by the raiſing of
the price in reſpect of money, of his particular commodity. The complaints of particular perſons ariſe, not from a deficiency of
money or counters in circulation; but from
their

their own want of property, want of skill, addrefs, or opportunity of getting more money; or perhaps only for want of frugality, in fpending more than their income or proper fhare. Anticipation is the grand fource of diftrefs and poverty, and is an evil that takes off much from the ufe of credit.

There is a limit to the vent and confumption of all forts of commodities. If, from an uncommon prolific feafon, or becaufe of a great demand at fome late market, or from any other caufe, as a new courfe of trade, &c. more of any fpecific commodity be produced, than what the ufual or neceffary confumption requires; the price of it will fall, and fome will be left on the owner's hands. Things growing out of fafhion will frequently undergo the fame fate; and in both cafes, the manufacturers and dealers in thofe commodities will be complaining, the workmen will be turned adrift, and all imputing their loffes and difappointments to the want of money in the country. But a greater plenty of money would not mend or better their condition; thofe who have it, will not be perfuaded to purchafe more of this or that commodity, than what their own wants, conveniency,

or

or fancy prompt them to; and thofe who cannot make fo much profit in their refpective profeffions as formerly, muft either turn themfelves fome other way, or be content to live more frugally. But all will not be wife in time; emulation in fhow is a powerful incentive; few can bear the thoughts of retrenching while it is yet time, and many finding themfelves upon the decline, will grow defperate and precipitate themfelves the fafter. In all great towns, bankruptcies will happen, and perhaps no where more frequent, than where wealth and money moft abound. Thefe evils, if upon the whole they be evils, are what the mines cannot cure, but are rather what have been introduced and foftered by them.

C H A P-

CHAPTER III.

Of EXCHANGES.

A S the accounts of particular perſons living in remote places, are frequently liquidated and diſcharged by *bills of exchange*, without the intervention of money; and this being a ſubject of importance, and not generally underſtood, excepting by particular merchants, it may not be amiſs in this place to give a brief account of the nature and uſe of exchanges.

I. *Bills of exchange, what.*

55. It hath been before obſerved, that the chief end or object of commerce betwixt nations, is a mutual exchange of commodities one with another; and this may be, and frequently is, carried to a great extent without the intervention of money. But neverthelefs the accounts are every where kept and ſtated in money; and it is almoſt unavoidable, but that in all great trading towns, there will be merchants, ſome having bullion owing to them in one place, ſome in another; ſome or other again that

are

are indebted to all thofe places, or to fome other place which is indebted to fome one of thofe; and fo, by a kind of chain, all trading countries become in fome fort accomptants with each other.

To avoid the charge, trouble and hazard of tranfporting bullion backwards and forwards, for the fupplying of thefe different occafions; the method of difcharging debts, by *bills of exchange* was introduced. This was an excellent * invention; thefe bills being

* This was the greateft fecurity to merchants both as to their perfons and effects, and confequently the greateft encouragement to commerce, and the greateft blow to defpotifm, of any thing that ever was invented. For, by this fort of correfpondence, merchants can imperceptibly convey away their effects when and wherever they pleafe; and this they will never fail doing, if they are in any wife molefted or threatened with danger. But at the fame time, that this is fo beneficial to commerce, and to liberty, both in certain degrees, ineftimable bleffings; it weakens the attatchments, and, as I may fay, the allegiances of tradefmen to their mother-country. And I fhould not, for many reafons, chufe to have my abode where the chief property and the chief rule was in mercantile hands. For, as an alloy to its very great advantages, there is fomething felfifh, ungenerous and illiberal in the nature and views of trade, that tends to debafe and fink the mind below its natural ftate. Somewhat of this muft be allowed to be the natural genius and bent of trade. Labourers or working people of all forts, are quite excluded out of the prefent confideration; and what is here faid is not intended as any reflection upon or difparagement to the other ranks of tradefmen: We live happily in a country, where various claffes of men by their daily intercourfes do, as it were, humanize, and benefit one the other a thoufand ways, and correct thofe errors and notions, which men confined to a particular fphere, are but too apt to fall into.

ing as fubfervient in foreign commerce, as coins are in home traffic; for by fhifting of debts and credits from one place to another, they fo far anfwer all the purpofes of money. Bills drawn betwixt places in the fame country, are called *Inland bills*; as thofe drawn between different countries, are called *Foreign bills of exchange.*

In all countries there are peculiar laws and cuftoms, relating to this bufinefs of exchanges, which merchants and others immediately concerned fhould be well verfed in. It is not my defign here to meddle with the practical part of this ufeful commerce, but to explain its theory or principles as briefly as I can. A part of what I here propofe is fo very well done to my hands in the *Britifh Merchant*, that I cannot do better in this place, than giving the following extract from that ufeful work.

" Suppofe the tenant in *Wiltfhire* is to
" pay for rent 100 *l.* to his landlord in *Lon-*
" *don*; and the *woollen-draper* in *London* is
" to pay the like fum to his *clothier* in *Wilt-*
" *fhire :* Both thefe debts may be paid,with
" out tranfmitting one farthing from the
" one place to the other, by bills of ex-
" change, or by exchanging one debtor for
" the

* Vol. III. fmall edition. p 97, 98, 99.

" the other, thus : That is, the tenant
" may receive his landlord's order to pay
" 100 *l.* to the *clothier* in the country ; and
" the *woollen-draper* may receive his *clothier's*
" order to pay the like sum to the landlord
" in town. These two orders are properly
" call'd bills of exchange ; the debts are
" exchanged by them, that is, the *woollen-*
" *draper* in town, instead of the tenant
" in the country, is become debtor to the
" landlord ; and the tenant in the country,
" instead of the *woollen-draper* in town, is
" become debtor to the *clothier :* And when
" these orders are comply'd with, the two
" debts between *London* and the country
" are discharged, without sending one shil-
" ling in specie from the one to the other."

" In like manner, the warehouse-man
" in *London* is indebted in 100 *l.* for stuffs,
" to the *weaver* in *Norwich* ; and the *li-*
" *nen-draper* in *Norwich* is indebted in the
" like sum to the *Hamborough* merchant in
" *London* ; both these debts may be paid
" by bills of exchange, or by the exchange
" of one debtor for the other, by placing
" one debtor in the other's stead ; that is,
" the warehouse-man may receive the or-
" der of his *weaver*, to pay 100 *l.* to the
" *Hamborough* merchant ; and the *linen-*
" *draper*

" *draper* may receive the order of the *Ham-*
" *borough* merchant to pay the like fum to
" the *weaver*. Thefe orders are bills of
" exchange ; the debtor in one place, is
" changed for the debtor in the other : and
" thus both debts may be paid, without
" fending one fingle fhilling in fpecie from
" the one city to the other."

   " If the debts reciprocally due between
" *London* and *Norwich*, are equal ; whe-
" ther they are 100 *l.* or 10,000 *l.* they
" may be all difcharged in this manner by
" bills of exchange, without fending any
" money in *fpecie* from the one to the
" other."

   " But if the debts due from both places
" are not equal, then only the fame quan-
" tity of debts on both fides, can be paid
" by bills of exchange. The ballance muft
" be fent in money from the city, from
" whence the greateft fums are due. For *Nature of*
" example : If by the trade between *London* *a ballance*
" and *Norwich*, the former owes 10,000 *l.* *in trade.*
" to the latter, and the latter no more than
" 9000 *l.* to the former ; it is manifeft, that
" only the debts of 9000 *l.* on each fide
" can be difcharg'd by bills of exchange ;
" the ballance of 1000 *l.* muft be fent ei-
" ther from *London* or fome other place in-
                   " debted

2

" debted to *London*, to even the accompt
" between both the cities."

" Let us fuppofe then, that to fend and

The occa-
fion of the
exchange
rifing to one
fide or
other.

" infure 1000 *l.* in fpecie to *Norwich,* would
" coft 5 *l.* or 10 *s. per Cent.* which of the
" debtors in *London* would be willing to
" be at this charge ? It is natural to believe
" that every one will endeavour to fhift it
" off from himfelf, that every one will en-
" deavour to pay his money by a bill of
" exchange ; it is natural to believe that
" every one, rather than ftand the coft and
" hazard of fending 100 *l.* in fpecie, would
" pay 100 *l.* 5 *s.* in *London* for a *debtor* in
" *Norwich*, upon condition that the *Nor-*
" *wich* debtor fhould pay 100 *l.* for him
" in that city. By which means the *Nor-*
" *wich* debtor would pay his debt of 100 *l.*
" in *London* with lefs than that fum, while
" the *London* debtor would be obliged to
" give more than that fum for the pay-
" ment of 100 *l.* in *Norwich.* And if fuch
" for years together were the courfe of ex-
" change between *London* and *Norwich*,
" there could be no queftion to which of
" the two cities a fum muft be fent in fpecie
" to pay the ballance ; that city undoubtedly
" pays the ballance that gives more than
" the par, that undoubtedly receives the
                                    " ballance

" ballance that gives lefs than the par for
" the bills of èxchange. The courfe of *Courfe of exchange*
" exchange in this cafe would fufficiently *decides the*
" decide, that the ballance of trade is on *ballance of*
" the fide of that city that procures bills of *trade.*
" exchange upon the moft eafy terms."

Foreign exchanges further explained.

56. The above example taken between two *Englifh* towns, explains the theory of exchanges very diftinctly. And from hence it may be eafily conceived, how the bufinefs of exchange may be carried on between any number of foreign towns. As, fuppofe that *London* is indebted to *Paris* in a fum of 100,000 ounces; *Paris* in a like fum to *Hamborough*; *Hamborough* in the fame fum to *Leghorn*; *Leghorn* to *Amfterdam*; *Amfterdam* in the like fum to *London*. All thefe feveral debts may be cancelled and difcharged by *bills of exchange*, without the tranfportation of one ounce of bullion or one penny of money. For inftance, *London* difcharges its debt at *Paris*, by a bill drawn upon *Amfterdam*; *Amfterdam* pays this bill by another drawn upon *Leghorn*; *Leghorn* again draws upon *Hamborough*; and laftly, by this rotation the debt from *Paris* to *Hamborough* becomes likewife dif-

I   charged;

charged; and all the above named towns
refpectively are cleared of all accounts with
each other. And the feveral debts above
fuppofed being equal, the debts of the refpective places will be difcharged with the
exchange at *par*, or without lofs or gain
to either. But as all the above towns may
have mutual accounts, each with all the
reft, and with many others; the real practice of exchange branches out into an immenfe labyrinth, not eafily unfolded without
much experience and application.

II. PAR *of exchange, what.*

57. The exchange is faid to be at *par* or
even, between two places, when a given fum
paid in the one, will purchafe a bill for the
like or a fum of the fame intrinfic value, to
be received in the other. To avoid all ambi-
guity, the feveral accounts in the preceding
article were ftated in ounces. But as all countries keep and ftate their accounts in their own
money, and moft places have peculiar coins
of their own; this makes it neceffary that
merchants, who are citizens of the world
in a ftricter fenfe than any other, fhould
know exactly the true proportional values
of the monies of all countries in refpect of
one another; that is, how much fine filver,

or

or fine gold, if the accompts are kept in
gold, are contained in the refpective ftandards or monies of the feveral countries to
or with which they traffic. Thefe proportions being known and ftated, the monies
of the world are thereby in effect reduced
to one common ftandard; and it may be
readily feen, how much of the money of one
country is an equivalent to, or contains an
equal quantity of filver with, a given fum
in another country.

The equality of filver, expreffed by different denominations of coins, conftitutes
what is ufually called the *par of exchange*
betwixt any two countries. In ftating this
par, fome particular fpecie or fum of the
money in one country, is ufually made the
unit or *integer*, which always remains fixed
and unalterable; and the proportion or equality is expreffed in fpecie of a fmaller value
of the other country; and it is in thefe
fpecie that the price is expreffed as the exchange varies: As if the exchange betwixt
London and *Paris* be reckoned in *pence* and
ecu's, and a *French ecu* contains as much
filver as there is in 29¼ *pence fterling*; then
the *ecu* is the *unit*, and 29¼ is the *par* of
exchange betwixt *London* and *Paris*. In
the mercantile language of exchange, that

country wherein the unit is eſtabliſhed, as in the above inſtance *Paris* in reſpect of *London*, is ſaid to give the *certain* for the *uncertain* ; as *London* again gives to *Paris* the uncertain for the certain. *London* gives the *certain* for the *uncertain*, that is, the *pound ſterling* for their *ſchillings*, to *Holland*, *Flanders* and *Hamborough* ; and to *France*, *Spain*, *Portugal* and *Italy*, *London* gives an uncertain number of pence, as the exchange governs, for a certain ſum in their money.

Thoſe who are not accuſtomed to this buſineſs, are apt to be in doubt whether the exchange riſing, for inſtance, be in our favour or againſt us. This doubt may be always cleared by this ſhort rule : The higher the exchange between any two countries is, the more it is in favour of that wherein the unit or invariable ſum is eſtabliſhed ; and the lower, the more in its disfavour. Thus, the higher is the exchange betwixt *London* and *Amſterdam*, the more is it in favour of *London*, as then the more *Dutch* ſchillings are given for the pound ſterling. On the contrary, the higher is the exchange between *London* and *Paris*, the more is it againſt *London*, as then the *French ecu* exchanges for a greater number of pence ſterling.

III.

III. *The true par of the exchange between different countries, difficult to be afcertained.*

58. Thofe who have made the proper experiments, find that moft of the foreign mints are very inaccurate ; and this makes it difficult to afcertain what are the precife values in refpect of one another, of the legal monies of different countries; and this is all that is ufually aimed at by the calculators of the *par of exchanges.* But this knowledge, if it could be obtained with ever fo much precifion, would be of very little fervice to the merchant, as the ftate of the coins in moft places now ftands. What the merchant muft regard, is, the amount in bullion of what he ufually receives in confideration of a given fum *of money.*

If the ballance due from any country, be ufually remitted in coins, and thofe coins be wore or otherwife diminifhed below the legal ftandard ; this will make a feeming difference in the true *par*, and the exchange in appearance will be againft that country when it is really even.

If in any country, gold be over-rated with refpect to filver, this will naturally drain away its filver coin, and gold coins

I 3   will

will become moſt current in large payments:
In this caſe, the merchant will make gold
his ſtandard, and rate the exchange accordingly. This will create a difference from
the nominal par of the exchange, which will
be more or leſs, according as gold is more
or leſs over-rated; and with this cauſe of
over-rating gold, the lightneſs of the coins
both gold and ſilver will alſo co-operate, in
proportion to the quantities of them exported; from both which cauſes the difference
between the true and nominal par may be
very conſiderable.

Theſe obſervations may ſerve to diſpel
the gloomy apprehenſions which ſome are
apt to entertain, from the courſe of exchange in general appearing ſo much againſt
England; and they alſo plainly ſhew that
the courſe of exchange betwixt different
countries, is not ſo critical and exact a rule
for meaſuring the ballance of trade, as is
commonly imagined; ſince it is hardly poſ-
ſible to aſcertain what is the *true par*. But
the exportation of bullion, is a certain ſign of
the exchange being really in favour of that
country to which it is ſent; and the variations in the exchanges, point alſo the variations in the ballance of trade; though,
in general, the rate of the exchange at a
particular

particular time, is fcarce fufficient for determining on which fide the ballance then
turns.

IV. *Courfe of exchange, what.*

59. The price at a certain time and place,
of bills of exchange for given fums drawn
upon another place, is called the *courfe of
exchange* between thofe two places at that
time; and this is frequently different from
the PAR, and more or lefs than an equivalent in fine filver or fine gold is to be paid
in one place, for a given fum to be received
in the other. Thus, fuppofing the par of
exchange betwixt *London* and *Paris* to be
$29\frac{1}{4}$ pence fterling for a *French* ecu; it
might happen at one time that a bill upon
Paris might be purchafed at *London*, at the
rate of 28 pence for an ecu; and that at
another time no bill could be had under
$30\frac{1}{2}$ or 31 pence.

As the ballance of accounts between the
feveral trading nations of the world, muft
be continually varying, and frequently fhifting to different fides; fo the courfe of exchange will be ever fluctuating, and it will
be more advantageous to make remittances
through certain channels at one time, and
by different ways at another. But as it

I 4   would

would be difficult for the grofs body of merchants to unravel thefe intricate clues, and to
find out and fupply each other's wants and
conveniences; particular perfons apply themfelves to this bufinefs, and *drawing* and *re-
mitting* by bills of exchange is it felf a diftinct trade. The *remitter* * or trader in bills
of exchange, muft have a real ftock or credit
in the feveral places with which he corre-
fponds; for bills, ftrictly fpeaking, pay no
debts; they only transfer credit from one place
to another; and whenever the demand for
bills to one place, are greater than the remitters can anfwer by their credit or ftock in
other places, they muft then tranfport as much
bullion as will fatisfy their correfpondents.
But the principal fkill of a remitter confifts in finding where and when bullion will
fetch moft, or where credit or bills are to
be had cheapeft, and where and when to
transfer this credit to moft advantage. For
bills of exchange being fubftitutes for bullion, are themfelves as much a commodity
as bullion, or any thing elfe; and the dealers
in them make their profits in the very fame
way

---

* Dealers in bills of exchange are in general terms ufually
called *remitters*: But with refpect to a particular tranfaction,
he who fells a bill, to be paid by his correfpondent in another
place, is called the *drawer*; and he who buys the faid bill,
and fends it abroad to have the value received by a fourth
perfon, is called the *remitter*.

way that other merchants do, by obferving the advantages of different markets.

V. *Price of bullion how influenced.*

60. A demand for bills upon a particular place, raifes their prices, as in other cafes; and when thefe prices have got up to a certain degree above par, the price of bullion will be alfo advanced above the ftandard of the country. For, dearnefs of bills caufes a demand for bullion to be exported, and in proportion of the demand to the ftock in the market, the price of bullion will be raifed. To take advantages when and wherever they offer, is the objeƐt and bufinefs of commerce. Again, by tranfporting of bullion the price of bills will be lowered; that again will gradually lower the price of bullion, until the prices of each are again brought to a par. The price of bills may be reduced below par; but bullion can never be lower than the eftablifhed ftandard, the mint being always open to receive it at the ftandard or mint price.

VI. *National intereſt, how influenced by the courſe of exchange.*

61. It feems, upon the firft view of the thing, that a country which oweth a ballance to another, muft pay a præmium upon

all

all the bills that pafs between them.   As,
fuppofing that in the accounts betwixt *England* and *Holland,* we owe the *Dutch* an
100,000 ounces, and that they owe us
90,000 ounces ; and fuppofing alfo that this
ballance of 10,000 ounces which we owe
to them, brings the exchange againſt us
one *per cent.*   It ſeems, I ſay, as if we
muſt pay this one *per cent.* not merely upon the ballance of 10,000, but upon the
whole 100,000 ; and on the other hand,
that we fhall receive fhort from them one
per cent. upon the whole 90,000 which
they owed us ; that is, that we muſt pay
the *Dutch* 101,000, whilſt they will difcharge their debt to us with 89,100 ; fo
that our whole loſs, upon the above fup-
poſitions, amounts to 1,900.   This at firſt
view ſeems to be the exact ſtate of the caſe ;
but upon examining this matter a little
cloſer, I think, it will appear that the loſs to
England by the exchange, is ordinarily no
more than what falls upon the ballance of
10,000.   Suppoſe the whole account at
London to ſtand betwixt two perſons, both
Engliſhmen;   *B* at *London* oweth *D* at *Amſterdam* an 100,000 ; *C* another *Dutchman*
at *Amſterdam* oweth *A* at *London* 90,000.
B pays to *A* 91,000 for for a bill upon *C*
to

to pay *D* 90,000; by this tranſaction the 90,000 *Dutch* debt at *London* is quite cleared, and what *B* loſt was gained by *A*. If the affair had been tranſacted at *Amſterdam*, the gain would have fallen to the ſhare of the debtor *C*, and the loſs on the creditor *D*; for *C* with 89,100 would have purchaſed of *D* a bill for 90,000 upon *B*. But although affairs of this kind are always tranſacted between ſeveral perſons, yet at laſt it comes to the ſame thing; and the whole gains, ſo far as bills will reach in liquidating the accounts, falls to the creditors on one ſide of the water, and to the debtors on the other. In the caſe above ſuppoſed, if ſome of the *Dutch* creditors reſide at *London*, or ſome of the *Engliſh* creditors at *Amſterdam*, this will turn the ſcale to the prejudice of *England*. Theſe obſervations plainly ſhew, that any calculations of national profit or loſs from the courſe of exchange, muſt needs be very precarious. Yet is it almoſt certain that by theſe tranſactions, that country will ſuſtain ſome loſs againſt which the exchange bears; and there is no other way of bringing the ballance even, but by the exportation of goods or bullion.

VII. *The courfe of exchange influenced by*
various caufes.

62. A demand for bills upon a particular place, may proceed from various caufes;
but thefe are chiefly reducible to the ballance of trade upon the whole, or between
particular places.   Bullion, like other commodities, traverfes through different climes,
and is ever of leaft value where it moft a-
bounds.   *Spain* and *Portugal* being the
chief fources from whence this commodity
is drawn to the reft of *Europe*, it is there
cheapeft and their chief ftaple ; and hence,
in the ufual phrafe, the ballance of trade
and the courfe of exchange will be every
where againft them.   This is natural, and
is no more to their prejudice, than it would
be to the *Englifh* to have the ballance againft
them, if the money of *Europe* was tin ; as
would then be the cafe, becaufe we have
the moft confiderable mines of that metal.
In like manner, and for the fame caufe, it
is natural that the ballance of trade, and
with it the courfe of exchange, between
the more fouthern and the northern parts of
Europe, fhould be in favour of the latter;
and this in general is the matter of fact.

The

The bufinefs of exchange between *England* and *Germany*, and the northern countries, is chiefly tranfacted at *London* and
Amfterdam. The courfe of exchange then
between us and *Holland*, indicates how the
ftate of accounts ftands between us and all
thofe countries in general, but not in refpect of any one in particular. The ballance of our trade to *Holland* may be greatly
in our favour, and yet the exchange to *Amfterdam* be generally againft us; both which
are fuppofed to be matters of fact. Our
debt to foreigners operates in the fame manner as a ballance of trade againft us, to the
whole amount of the dividends owing to
them; and the fame is true as to all foreign
fubfidies If thofe dividends paid to foreigners contribute to enlarge our manufacturies and exports, our lofs is thereby alle-
viated; but if they do not, that is, if our
commerce remains in *ftatu quo*, we are lofers to their whole amount, and that equally
whether their produce is exported in goods
or bullion; if they are fent in goods, they
prevent fo much bullion from coming to
us. This is an affecting confideration, and
the fources of this country muft be prodi-
gious great to be enabled to fuftain fo great

a

a burden. But let us not be too fecure, and neglect a matter of fo much importance.

VIII. *Bullion is not exported till the exchange is at a certain limit from par.*

63. Merchants always prefer bills of exchange, whilft they are to be had at moderate rates, before bullion or cafh, which with them is the fame thing; and bullion is never tranfported from one place to another, till the exchange is at a certain diftance from *par*; and this diftance is again limited by the expence of tranfporting bullion, wherein is included, befides the freight, commiffion and infurance. And hence, the whole fluctuation in the courfe of exchange is very different between different places. Betwixt *London* and *Paris*, the exchange muft vary about $\frac{3}{4}$ *per cent.* from *par*, before bullion, at leaft in any quantity, will be fent from either fide. The freight of bullion from *London* to *Calais* is about $\frac{1}{4}$ *per cent.* from thence to *Paris* about $\frac{1}{8}$, infurance in the whole to *Paris* about $\frac{3}{8}$, which make altogether $\frac{3}{4}$ *per cent.*; and fo much at leaft the exchange muft be againft us, before any bullion will be fent from *London* to *Paris*; and it muft be as much in our favour,

vour, before any bullion will be brought
hither from thence.   By this reckoning, the
exchange betwixt *London* and *Paris* may
vary $1\frac{1}{2}$ *per cent.* before gold or filver will
move towards either fide.   To *Amflerdam*,
the expence of tranfporting bullion from
London, is lefs than to *Paris* ; to fome other
places, this expence is greater, and accordingly the exchange varies lefs or more between different countries; becaufe, as hath
been before obferved, the tranfportation of
bullion keeps the courfe of exchange within
a certain limit.

Bills are frequently drawn, and bullion
carried, between two places that are even
in their accounts, to pay debts in a third
place.   If the exchange betwixt *Calais* and
Paris be againft *Calais*, and it be at par directly between *Calais, London* and *Paris* ;
a merchant at *Calais* will pay his debts at
Paris by a bill upon *London* : And if the
exchange betwixt him and *Paris*, and betwixt *London* and *Paris* will permit, our
Calais merchant will purchafe a *London* bill
by fending gold thither, inftead of fending
it directly to *Paris*.   It is in finding and taking the advantages of the feveral markets,
that the myftery of this traffic by exchange
doth principally confift.

This

This ſhort account may ſuffice to explain the general theory of exchanges ; a theory curious in it ſelf, and the practical part is extreamly uſeful for the purpoſes of foreign commerce. But to meddle with that, doth not fall within the compaſs of my deſign.

The End of the FIRST PART.

A N

ESSAY

UPON

MONEY and COINS.

PART II.

WHEREIN IS SHEWED,

That the ESTABLISHED STANDARD of MONEY fhould not be *violated* or *altered*, under any pretence whatfoever.

LONDON,

Printed: Sold by G. HAWKINS at *Milton's Head,* by the *Middle Temple-Gate,* in *Fleet-ftreet.*
M.DCC.LVIII.

TO THE RIGHT HONOURABLE

HENRY BILSON LEGGE,

One of the LORDS of the TREASURY,
CHANCELLOR and Under-Treasurer of
the EXCHECQUER, and one of the Lords
of His MAJESTY's Moft Honourable
PRIVY-COUNCIL.

S I R,

THE fubject of the fol-
lowing fheets, peculi-
arly requires and deferves the
protection of an able and honeft patron; for, important
as it is to the public welfare,
few men perfectly underftand
it, and too many have indu-
ftrioufly perplexed it, fome
perhaps, for private views of
their own.

The free accefs which your
friendfhip hath allowed me,
hath given me many oppor-
tunities

tunities of obferving the clofe application you are always ready to give to every fubject, in which the intereft of your country is concerned; and of admiring the happy talent you poffefs of explaining thofe which are of the moft intricate nature, with the greateft clearnefs, ftrength, and precifion.

Permit me therefore, Sir, to infcribe the following tract to you, as a token of the affection I bear to your private as well as of the refpect I pay to your public character.

I am,

S I R,

Your moft faithful
and obedient fervant,

THE AUTHOR.

THE

PREFACE.

IN the preceding part of this eſſay, I have endeavoured to explain the theory and nature of money, in ſuch a manner, as to leave no room for any doubts or difficulties concerning it. But notwithſtanding all my care, I do not expect univerſal approbation : Such are the infinite diverſities and warpings of the human mind; and ſuch are the inadvertencies, perverſeneſſes and prejudices of many, that unanimity in any one point is hardly to be expected. And unfortunately, money is a ſubject wherein men in general have given themſelves the leaſt trouble of enquiry ; and yet a ſubject upon which they think themſelves beſt qualified and beſt entitled to decide : A ſub-

je(ct

ject upon which, more jejune, inco-
herent and dangerous pofitions have
been held, and more glaring abfurdi-
ties advanced, than, perhaps, upon any
other whatfoever. But truth is mighty;
and to as many as can think freely
for themfelves, and have confidered
what I have already laid before them,
I hope that what is here offered will
appear evident and inconteftible.

The defign of this fecond part is
a very arduous and important one :
It is to defend and preferve every
man's right and property ; to preferve unfullied the national faith,
honour and credit ; to preferve a
reign hitherto diftinguifhed by equal
laws and equal adminiftration of juftice, from a blot that would remain
to all pofterity : To vindicate and
defend all thefe, I fay, from an af-
faffination in the dark, by a debafement of the long eftablifhed ftandard
of property. Some of our opponents
in

in this queſtion, no doubt, mean well;
and perſiſt in their errors for want of
underſtanding the ſubjeȼt, and that
perhaps too, only from their not having duly conſidered it. Others, it is
to be feared, ſeek only their own private gain; in competition with which,
it is not to be expeȼted that with
ſuch men, either the diſhonour or
diſtreſſes of their country, ſhould
have much weight.

Towards the cloſe of the laſt century, this country ſwarmed with pro-
jeȼtors, who were for debaſing the
ſtandard of money. Theſe were fully anſwered, if they would have
taken an anſwer, by the great Mr.
LOCKE, as to the point then in debate.
The very ill ſtate of our coin at that
time, might miſlead many well meaning people into wrong notions, as to
the means of redreſſing that great
evil, which the nation then labour'd
under: But, after what was then

I

ſaid

said and done, to have the same false doctrine maintained and propagated at this day, is truly matter of astonishment.

Mr. *Locke* seems to have been called to this work, before he had considered the subject at large ; and although he was perfectly right as to the main point then in debate ; yet it must be owned that his tracts upon this subject, though voluminous, if considered as a system of the theory of money, are very deficient and imperfect, if not in some places bordering upon mistakes. It is with much reluctance, but it is with a very honest design, that I say thus much to the disparagement of this truly eminent author : It is to guard the reader against trusting too far to a guide, that would scarce be able to conduct him clear of many obstacles that might fall in his way.

I have endeavoured to fupply this
defect, to remove all thofe difficulties which feem to have mifled people upon this delicate, complex, and
important fubject, and to frame the
whole ftructure upon felf-evident
principles. It fhould not be here
concealed that we have on our fide
of the queftion, fome of the moft
diftinguifhed names that this or any
other country hath produced : No
lefs than the great Lord BURLEIGH,
Lord HALIFAX, Lord SOMMERS, Sir
THOMAS ROWE, Mr. LOCKE, Sir ISAAC
NEWTON, MARTIN FOLKES, Efq; &c.
Some of thefe are quoted, in their
own words, in the firft enfuing chapter ; and it is but fair and equitable,
that thofe who will not or cannot
think for themfelves, fhould pay a
due regard to fuch venerable and
great authorities.

Before

Before I conclude, I ought in juſtice to acquaint the reader, that this tract was not undertaken from any apprehenſion, that our government now hath or is likely to have any deſign of altering our ſtandard ; it is rather with a view to the quiet of thoſe in power from the importunities of wrong-headed politicians, as well as to the ſafety of the whole from the intrigues of wily projectors.

THE

THE
CONTENTS.

CHAP. I.

CHAP.

C H A P. II.

PART II.

CHAPTER I.

*A summary account of all the altera-
tions that have been made in our
standard of money, from the* Norman *conquest to the present time,
with the opinions of some very eminent men upon those kinds of measures.*

THAT the reader may comprehend
at one view, the several adulterations
that have been made in our money
standard, ever since the *Norman* conquest;
I have inserted the following table, computed to my hand by the late learned
MARTIN FOLKES, Esq; and printed in his
curious *Table of* English *silver coins*, &c.
page 142 ; to which I have added the proportion which, in our coins, fire gold bore
to fine silver, at the respective times therein
specified, fine silver being reckoned unity
or 1.

B   A TA-

1. A TABLE fhewing at one view, the feveral adulterations that have been made in the ftandard of our money, from the *Norman* conqueft to this time.

Years of the kings reign, and *A. D.*	Finenefs of the filver.	Weight of 20 fh. in tale. Troy-wt.	Value in prefent money.			Proportion.	Fine gold to fine filver.
	oz. dwts	oz. dwts. gr.	l.	s.	d.		
Conqueft 1066	11 2	11* 5	2	18	1½	2.906	} No
28 Edw. I. 1300	11 2	11 2 5	2	17	5	2.871	} gold.
18 Edw. III. 1344		10 3	2	12	5¼	2.622	12.583
20 ditto 1346		10	2	11	8	2.583	11.571
27 ditto 1353		9	2	6	6	2.325	11.158
13 Hen. IV. 1412		7 10	1	18	9	1.937	
4 Edw. IV. 1464		6	1	11		1. 55	10.331
18 Hen.VIII. 1527		5 6 16	1	7	6¼	1.378	11.267
34 ditto 1543	10	5	1	3	3¼	1.163	10.435
36 ditto 1545	6	5		13	11½	0.698	6.818
37 ditto 1546	4	5		9	3¼	0.466	5.
3 Edw. VI. 1549	6	3 6 16		9	3¼	0.466	5.151
5 ditto 1551	3	3 6 16		4	7½	0.232	2.011
6 ditto 1552	11 1	4	1	0	6¼	1.028	11. 05
1 Mary 1553	11	4	1	0	5¼	1.024	11. 05
2 Eliz. 1560	11 2	4	1	0	8	1.033	11. 1
43 ditto 1601	11 2	3 17 10	1			1.	10.905

Obfervations on the foregoing TABLE.

2. From the above table, it appears that the ftandard of money remained unaltered here, for the fpace of 234 years after the con-

* *N. B.* The *Saxon* or *Tower* pound, which was then the common weight, and continued to be the money weight till the 18th year of *Henry* VIII. was but 11 oz. 5 dwt troy, fo that 20 fhillings in tale was then exactly a pound in weight.

conqueft; during which period, a pound in money was alfo a pound in weight. After the old ftandard had been once broke upon, it was again and again curtailed ; however, they obferved fome meafure, and the old ftandard of finenefs was preferved, till the 34 *Hen.* VIII. This king afterwards re-duced the ftandard to lefs than one third of what it had been for 63 years, before he began to tamper with it; and in the fifth year of the reign of his fon. young king *Edward,* the money ftandard was reduced to lefs than one fourth of what it is at pre-fent; and they were fo extravagant as to raife up filver at the mint to about half the value of gold. What were the immediate effects of thofe wild meafures, hiftorians have not been particular in informing us ; but they muft needs have been calamitous in a thoufand refpects : That the evils were very grievous, may be conjectured from the bold ftep taken the very next year, of increafing at once the ftandard betwixt four and five times : A meafure fo extraor-dinary, that it muft have been attended with infinite diforders, if the people in their dealings, during that fhort dark period of debafing the money, had not en-deavoured to have kept to the ftandard, as it was in the preceding times. Befides the

unavoidable evil of hoarding, or tranſport-
ing of the old coins at under rates, and more
eſpecially the gold ones, to the very great
loſs of the nation; it appears by the following proclamation, that the people either
refuſed to bring their goods to market, or
not to ſell them but at very high rates.

" 3. * In 1550, *Sept.* 22. A procla-
" mation was ſet forth, by the which it
" was commanded, 1. That no kind of
" victual, no wax, tallow, candles, nor no
" ſuch thing ſhould be carried over, ex-
" cept to *Calais,* putting in ſureties to go
" thither. 2. That no man ſhould buy
" or ſell the ſelf-ſame things again, except
" broakers, who ſhould not have more than
" ten quarters of grain at once. 3. That
" all parties ſhould divide themſelves into
" hundreds, rapes, and wapentakes, to
" look in their quarters what ſuperfluous
" corn were in every barn, and appoint it to
" be ſold at a reaſonable price. Alſo that
" one of them muſt be in every market to
" ſee the corn brought. Furthermore, who-
" ever ſhipped over any thing aforeſaid, to
" the parts beyond ſea, or *Scotland,* after
" eight

* FOLKE's *table of* Engliſh *ſilver coins,* page 35. We are
much obliged to this learned author for the great pains he
took in gathering many curious anecdotes relating to this
ſubject.

" eight days following the publication of
" the proclamation, fhould forfeit his fhip,
" and the ware therein, half to the lord of
" the franchize, and half to the finder
" thereof ; whofo bought to fell again after
" the day aforefaid, fhould forfeit all his
" goods, farms, and leafes, to the ufe, one
" half of the finder, the other of the king ;
" who fo brought not in corn to market as
" he was appointed, fhould forfeit 10 *l*.
" except the purveyors took it up, or it
" were fold to his neighbours." *King's
Journal.*

    " It further appears alfo, by the king's *Edw*. VI.
" journal, that on the 19th of *October*, 1550,   1551.
" prices had been fet of all kind of grains,
" butter, cheefe, and poultry ware, by a pro-
" clamation ;" and that, on the 20th of the
following *November*, " there had been let-
" ters fent down to the gentlemen of every
" fhire, for the obfervation of the laft pro-
" clamation concerning corn, becaufe there
" came none to the markets, commanding
" them to punifh the offenders : " But that
" upon letters written back by the fame,
" the fecond proclamation had been abo-
" lifhed, on the 29th of the fame month."

To thefe authorities collected by this learned gentleman, I beg leave to add fome of his fentiments upon this fubject, in his * own words.

" 4. All ways had before this been tried,
" and all means had been found ineffectual,
" for the keeping up the value, and fup-
" porting the currency of the bafe mo-
" ney:—" " † It was now found by ex-
" perience that gold and filver had, by the
" common confent of all people throughout
" the civilized parts of the world, acquired
" certain real and proper values : and that
" in fuch a nation as this, not deftitute even
" then of all commerce with ftrangers, it
" was impoffible that the arbitrary value
" fet upon pieces of bafe metal could, for
" any confiderable time, fupply the want
" of the filver that ufed to be contained in
" the pieces of the fame denominations.
" Whatever names were given to thofe
" pieces of bafe metal, or by whatever au-
" thority their imaginary value was fup-
" ported ; the people would either not bring
" their provifions at all to the markets, to
" exchange them for fuch money, or
" would there fell them at much higher
                                " rates

* FOLKES's *table of* Englifh *filver coins,* p. 35.
† Ibid. p. 36.

" rates than before : as the nominal fums
" they received for their goods, would not
" now purchafe them the fame conveniencies
" elfewhere, as the fame nominal fums of
" better money had formerly done.   It was
" therefore judged abfolutely neceffary to
" reform and to amend the coin ; the affair
" was very ferioufly confidered, and the
" work was undertaken and carried on,
" with fo much diligence and vigour, that
" within a few months a reformation of the
" money was brought about, truly memo-
" rable, and no lefs remarkable than the
" former abufes of it had been : for the
" new pieces that were coined before the
" end of this year 1551, were of more
" than four times the value of thofe of the
" fame denominations, that had been coined
" in the former months of the fame. † "

B 4   5. The

† In p. 30, 31. of the above work, are two remarkable
paffages relating to this fubject, extracted out of two fermons
preached before the king, by the truly excellent bifhop
LATIMER, in *March* 1549. In the firft he fays, " We have
" now a pretty little fhilling, indeed a very pretty one. I
" have but one I think in my purfe, and the laft day I had
" put it away almoft for an old groat, and fo I truft fome
" will take them. The finenefs of the filver I cannot fee :
" but therein is printed a fine fentence, *Tim:r Domini*
" *fons vitæ vel fapientiæ*." In the next fermon, he fays,
" Thus they burdened me ever with fedition. And wot ye
" what ? I chanced in my laft fermon to fpeak a merry word
" of the new fhilling, to refrefh my auditory, how I was
" like

5. The mifchiefs occafioned by thefe bafe
coins could not be fully fubdued till queen
Elizabeth's time; and the conquering of
that monfter, as fhe called it, was deemed
by that illuftrious queen, as one of the moft
glorious acts of her reign. Queen *Mary*
fettled the ftandard at 11 oz. fine, and 60
fhillings were cut out of the pound troy.
Queen *Elizabeth*, in her fecond year brought
the ftandard into its antient finenefs of 11
oz.

" like to put away my new fhilling for an old groat.
" I was therein noted to fpeak feditioufly.——I have now
" gotten one fellowe more, a companion of fedition, and
" wot you who is my fellowe? *Efay* the prophet. I fpake
" but of a little prettie fhilling, but he fpeaketh to *Jerufalem*
" after another fort, and was fo bold as to meddle with
" their coynes. Thou proud, thou haughty city of *Jeru-*
" *falem : Argentum tuum verfum eft in fcoriam*, thy filver is
" turned into, what? into teftions? *fcoriam*, into drofs.
" Ah feditious wretch, what had he to do with the mint?
" Why fhould he not have left that matter to fome mafter
" of policy to reprove? thy filver is drofs, it is not
" fine, it is counterfeit, thy filver is turned; thou hadft
" good filver What pertained that unto *Efay?* marry he
" efpied a piece of divinity in that policy, he threatneth
" them God's vengeance for it. He went to the root of the
" matter, which was covetoufnefs; he efpied two points in
" it, that either it came of covetoufnefs, which became
" him to reprove: or elfe that it tended to the hurt of poore
" people; for the naughtinefs of the filver was the occafion
" of dearth of all things in the realm. He imputeth it to
" them as a crime. He may be called a mafter of fedition
' indeed. Was not this a feditious fellow; to tell them this
" even to their faces?" I have cited thefe paffages at
large, becaufe they not only fhew in the cleareft manner,
this good bifhop's own fentiments of the pernicious confequence of the bafe money then current, but what moft probably was alfo the common notions and talk at that time.

oz. 2 dwts. and cut as before, juſt 60 ſhillings out of the pound troy. But in the 43d year of her reign, the ſtandard was debaſed once more, by cutting the ſaid pound into 62 ſhillings.

6. The above laſt alteration remains yet to be regretted, as now none of our coins are aliquot or even parts of our weights. For about 50 years before, whilſt the pound weight troy of ſilver, was cut into 60 ſhillings; the money pound being exactly 4 ounces, the crown-piece was one ounce, the ſhilling 4dwts. and the penny 8 grains. Had this ſtandard been continued, every one would have readily known, how much ſilver each piece of money ought to contain; and would naturally have led people to compare coins with weights, which probably would have produced long ago, ſome of the regulations now ſo much wanted in regard to money, and which would have ſaved this nation from great loſs and perplexity. It were to be wiſhed alſo, that our ſilver and gold coins were of the ſame fineneſs one with another; for then their reſpective values might have been the eaſier compared. This would now have been the caſe, if the ſilver ſtandard of 11 oz. fine had been continued, as it was ſet-

3   tled

tled by queen *Mary*. But thefe things cannot now be remedied, without rifquing a
much greater inconvenience; as it is dangerous to meddle in any wife with the ftand-
dard of money.

It is no wonder if amidft the various
fchemes for fupplying the neceffities of
king *Charles* I. that alfo of debafing the
coin fhould be taken into confideration :
But the miniftry feem to have been fully
convinced of the vanity of fuch projects, by
a * fpeech made at the council table in
July 1640 by Sir *Thomas Rowe*, of which
I have made the following extract.

" *My* LORDS,

" 7. Since it hath pleafed this honoura-
" ble table, to command, amongft others,
" my poor opinion concerning this weighty
" propofition of money ; I muft humbly
" crave pardon, if with that freedom that
" becometh my duty to my good and graci-
" ous mafter, and my obedience to your
" great commands, I deliver it fo."

                                        " I con-

* This fpeech is printed in *Rufhworth*'s collections for
July 1640 ; it is alfo printed among fome pofthumous
pieces of Sir *Robert Cotton*'s, as if made by him at the fame
place on *Sept.* 2, 1626. I believe there is a miftake as to
this laft date, which foever of thefe two renowned knights
was the real author.

" I conceive this intended project of en-
" feebling the coin, will intrench very
" far, both into the honour, juftice, and
" profit of the king."—— " *Vopifcus* faith,
" the fteps by which the (*Roman*) ftate de-
" fcended were vifible moft by the general
" alteration of their coins : And there is
" no furer fymptoms of confumption in
" ftate, than the corruption of money.—
" When *Henry* VIII. had gained as much
" of power and glory abroad, of love and
" obedience at home, as ever any ; he fuf-
" fered fhipwreck of all upon this rock.—
" To avoid the trouble of permutation,
" coins were devifed as a rule and mea-
" fure of merchandize and manufactories ;
" which if mutable, no man can tell either
" what he hath, or what he oweth ; no
" contract can be certain, and fo all com-
" merce both publick and private is de-
" ftroyed ; and men again enforced to per-
" mutation with things not fubject to will
" and fraud.

" The regulating of coin hath been left
" to the care of princes, who have ever
" been prefumed to be the fathers of the
" commonwealth ; upon their honours
" they are debtors and warranties of juftice
" to the fubject, in that behalf. They
" can-

" cannot, faith *Bodin*, alter the price of mo-
" nies to the prejudice of the fubjects,
" without incurring the reproach of *faux*
" *monnoyeurs*. And therefore ftories term
" *Philip le Bell*, for ufing it, *falfificateur de*
" *moneta. Integritas debet queri ubi vultus*
" *nofter imprimatur*, faid *Theodoret* the
" *Gothe* to his mint - mafter, *Quidnam*
" *erit tutum fi in noftra peccetur effige ?*
" Princes muft not fuffer their faces to
" warrant falfhood.—And I muft with in-
" finite comfort acknowledge, the care and
" juftice now of my good mafter, and your
" lordfhips wifdoms, that would not upon
" the information of fome few officers of
" the mint, before a free and careful de-
" bate, put in execution this project ;
" which I much (under your honours fa-
" vour) fufpect, would have taken away
" the tenth part of every man's due debt
" or rent already referved throughout the
" realm, not fparing the king ; which
" would have been little lefs than a fpecies
" of that which the *Roman* ftories call *ta-*
" *bulæ novæ*, from whence very often fe-
" ditions have fprung.
  " In this laft part, which is the difprofit
" that the enfeebling the coin will bring
" both to his majefty, and to the common-
                                        " wealth ;

" wealth ; I muſt diſtinguiſh the monies of
" gold and ſilver, as they are bullion and
" commodities, and as they are meaſures :
" The one, the † extrinſic quality, which
" is at the king's pleaſure, as all other
" meaſures to name ; the other, the in-
" trinſic quality of pure metal, which is
" in the merchant to value : As their mea-
" ſure ſhall be either leſſened or enlarged,
" ſo is the quantity of the commodity that
" is to be exchanged. If then the king
" ſhall cut his ſhilling or pound in money
" leſs then it was before, a leſs proportion
" of ſuch commodities as ſhall be exchanged
" for it, muſt be received : It muſt then of
" force follow, that all things of neceſſity,
" as victuals, apparel, and the reſt, as well
" as thoſe of pleaſure, muſt be enhanced.
" If then all men ſhall receive in their
" ſhillings and pounds, a leſs proportion of
" ſilver and gold than they did before this
" projected alteration ; and pay for what
                              " they

† The terms *extrinſic, intrinſic,* and *real* qualities or
values, are frequently to be met with in writers about coins.
But in general theſe are vague expreſſions : *intrinſic* and
real qualities, ſeem to be ſynominous terms ; and by *extrinſic* quality or value is meant I ſuppoſe, above, the rate or
ſeignorage paid at the mint for coinage. For coins made
gratis, or at the expence of the public, can have no extrinſic value above mere bullion.

" they buy at a rate enhanced, it muſt caſt
" upon all a double loſs.

" What the king will ſuffer by it in the
" rents of his lands, is demonſtrated enough
" by the alteration ſince the 18th of
" *Edward* III, when all the revenues of the
" crown came into the receipts, *pondere*
" *& numero*, after five groats the ounce ;
" which ſince that time, by the ſeveral
" changes of the ſtandard is come to five
" ſhillings, whereby the king hath loſt
" two third parts of his juſt revenues.

" In his cuſtoms, the book of rates be-
" ing regulated by pounds and ſhillings, his
" majeſty muſt loſe alike ; and ſo in all,
" and whatſoever monies that after this he
" ſhall receive : The profits by this change
" in coinage, cannot be much, nor per-
" manent, the loſs laſting.—And as his
" majeſty ſhall undergo all this loſs here-
" after in all his receipts, ſo ſhall he no
" leſs in all his diſburſements. The wages
" of his ſoldiers muſt be rateably advanced,
" as the money is decreaſed. This
" *Edward* III, as appeareth by the accounts
" of the wardrobe and exchequer, and all
" the kings after him were enforced to do,
" as oft as they leſſened the ſtandard of

3   " their

" their monies. What fhall be bought for
" his majefty's fervice, muft in like man-
" ner be enhanced on him. And as his
" majefty hath the greateft of receipts and
" iffues, fo muft he of neceffity tafte of
" the moft lofs by this device.

" It will deftroy or difcourage a great
" proportion of the trade in *England,* and
" fo impair his majefty's cuftoms ; for
" that part (being not the leaft) that paf-
" feth upon truft and credit will be over-
" thrown : For all men being doubtful of
" diminution hereby of their perfonal eftates,
" will call in their monies already out, and
" no man will part with that which is ly-
" ing by him, upon fuch apparent lofs as
" this muft bring. What damage may be-
" fal the ftate by fuch a fudden ftand of
" trade, is fubmitted to confideration. The
" monies both of gold and filver, formerly
" coined and abroad, being richer than thofe
" intended, will be tranfported ; which I
" conceive to be none of the leaft induce-
" ments that hath drawn fo many gold-
" fmiths to fide in this project, that they
" may be thereby factors for the ftrangers,
" who by the lownefs of minting (being but
" 2 *s.* the pound weight of filver, and 4 *s.*
                                    " for

" for gold; whereas with us, the one is
" 2 *s.* 6 *d.* and the other 5 *s.*) may make
" that profit beyond fea they cannot here,
" and fo his majefty's mint be unfet on
" work. And as his majefty fhall lofe ap-
" parently in the alteration of monies, a
" fourteenth in all the filver, and a twenty-
" fifth part in all the gold he after fhall re-
" ceive; fo fhall the nobility, gentry, and all
" others, in all their former fettled rents,
" annuities, penfions, and loans of money.
" The like will fall upon the labourers and
" workmen in their ftatute wages: And as
" their receipts are leffened hereby; fo are
" their iffues increafed, either by improv-
" ing all prices, or disfurnifhing the mar-
" ket, which muft neceffarily follow. For
" if in the 5 *Edward* VI. 3 *Mary,* and 4
" *Elizabeth,* as appeareth by their procla-
" mations, a rumour only of an alteration
" caufed thefe effects, and they punifhed
" the authors of fuch reports with imprifon-
" ment and pillory; it cannot be doubted,
" but the projecting a change muft be of far
" more confequence and danger to the ftate;
" and it is to be wifhed that the actors and
" the authors of fuch difturbances in the
" commonwealth at all times hereafter,
" might

" might undergo a punifhment proportion-
" able——.Experience hath taught us, that
" the enfeebling of coin is but a fhift for a
" while, as drink to one in a dropfy, to
" make him fwell the more : But the ftate
" was never thoroughly cured, as we faw
" in *Henry* the VIIIth's time, and the late
" queen, until the coin was made up again.

" I cannot then but conclude, my honour-
" able lords, that if the proportion of gold
" and filver to each other be wrought to
" that parity, by the advice of artifts, that
" neither may be too rich for the other ; that
" the mintage may be reduced to fome pro-
" portion of neighbour parts ; and the
" iffue of our native commodities may be
" brought to over-balance the entrance of
" the foreign, we need not feek any fhift, but
" fhall again fee our trade to flourifh, the
" mint, as the pulfe of the commonwealth,
" again to beat, and our materials, by in-
" duftry, to be mines of gold and filver to
" us ; and the honour, juftice and profit of
" his majefty (which we all wifh and work
" for) fupported."

8. The above excellent fpeech is fo clear
and full to the point, as to need no remarks.

C	It

It fhews that the nature of money, however it came to be fo much miftaken fince,
was formerly well underftood ; and by a
paffage in it, and in the † report of a com-
mittee appointed by the privy-council to
examine into the project of debafing the
coin, we learn that the faid project came from
fome officers of the mint, with whom were
alfo joined certain goldfmiths or money-
mongers : And to facilitate the fcheme, it appears, that thefe gentlemen did not fcruple
to make allegations that were falfe in point
of fact.   It will be fhewed hereafter, why
mint-mafters have an intereft in promoting
any alteration in the ftandard of money :
And although nothing that hath been here
or elfewhere faid, is intended as a reflection
upon any perfons of the prefent age, as I do
not think that they deferve fuch a cenfure ;
yet it may ferve as a ftanding caution to thofe
in power, not to truft too far to the opinions or gloffes of thofe, who may be inte-
refted in deceiving them.

The report above referred to, is too long
to be here inferted at full length ; but the
following extract, being part of the refult
of

† This report is printed in the forecited works of Sir
Robert Cotton's.

of the confultation then held at court, and drawn up with great ftrength and concife-nefs, I could not well omit.

9. " Gold and filver have a two fold ef-
" timation : In the *extrinfic*, as they are
" monies, they are the prince's meafures
" given to his people ; and this is a prero-
" gative of kings.   In the *intrinfic* they
" are commodities, valuing each other ac-
" cording to the plenty or fcarcity ; and fo
" all other commodities by them ; and that
" is the fole power of trade.

 " The meafures in a kingdom ought to
" be conftant : It is the juftice and honour
" of the king : For if they be altered, all
" men at that inftant are deceived in their
" precedent contracts, either for lands or
" money, and the king moft of all : For
" no man knoweth then, either what he
" hath, or what he oweth.

 " This made lord treafurer *Burleigh*, in
" 1573, when fome projectors had fet on
" foot a matter of this nature, to tell them
" that they were worthy to fuffer death, for
" attempting to put fo great a difhonour on
" the queen, and detriment and difcontent
" upon the people. For, to alter this pub-
" lic meafure, is to leave all the markets

" of the kingdom unfurnished ; and what
" will be the mischief, the proclamations
" of 5 *Edward* VI. 3 *Mary*, and 4 *Eli-*
" *zabeth*, will manifest ; when but a ru-
" mour of the like, produced that effect so
" far, that besides the faith of the princes
" to the contrary delivered in their edicts,
" they were inforced to cause the magi-
" strates in every shire respectively, to con-
" strain the people to furnish the markets
" to prevent a mutiny. To make this mea-
" sure then, at this time short, is to raise
" all prices, or to turn the money or mea-
" sure now current into disise or bullion :
" For who will part with any, while it is
" richer by seven in the hundred in the
" mass, than the new monies ; and yet of
" no more value in the market ?

" Hence of necessity, it must follow,
" that there will not in a long time be suf-
" ficient minted of the new to drive the
" exchange of the kingdom, and so all
" trade at one instant at a stand ; and in the
" mean time the markets unfurnished :
" which how it may concern the quiet of
" the state, is worthy care.

" And thus far as money is a *measure*.
" Now as it is a *commodity*, it is respected
                                           " and

" and valued by the intrinfic quality; and
" firft the one metal to the other.

" All commodities are prized by plenty
" or fcarcity, the one by the other: If
" then we defire our filver to buy gold, as
" it lately hath done, we muft let it be the
" cheaper, and lefs in proportion valued;
" and fo contrary: For one equivalent pro-
" portion in both, will bring in neither.
" We fee the proof thereof by the unufual
" quantity of *gold* brought lately to the
" mint by reafon of the price; for we rate
" it above all other countries, and gold
" may be bought too dear. To furnifh
" then this way the mint with both, is al-
" together impoffible.

" And at this time it was apparently
" proved, both by the beft *artifts*, and
" *merchants* beft acquainted with the *ex-
" change*, in both the examples of the mint-
" mafters, in the *rix-dollar* and *real of
" eight*, that filver here is of equal value,
" and gold above, with the foreign parts
" in the intrinfic; and that the *fallacy*
" prefented to the *lords* by the *mint-mafters*,
" is only in the *nomination* or extrinfic
" quality."

C 3 " But

" But if we defire both, it is not raifing
" of the value that doth it; but the *balan-*
" *cing* of *trade :* For buy we in more than
" we fell of other *commodities*, be the mo-
" ney never fo high prized, we muft part
" with it to make the difproportion even :
" If we fell more than we buy, the con-
" trary will *follow.*"

" And this is plain in *Spain*'s neceffities :
" For fhould that king advance to a double
" rate his *real of eight*, yet needing, by
" reafon of the barrennefs of his country,
" more of foreign wares than he can coun-
" tervail by exchange with his own, he muft
" part with his money, and gaineth no
" more by enhancing his coin, but that he
" payeth a higher price for the commodi-
" ties he buyeth ; if his work of raifing be
" his own.   But if we fhall make improve-
" ment of *gold* and *filver*, being the ftaple
" *commodity* of his ftate ; we then, advan-
" cing the price of his, abafe to him our
" own commodities."

" To fhape this kingdom to the fafhion·
" of the *Netherlanders*, were to frame a royal
" *monarch* by a fociety of merchants. Their
" country is a continual fair, and fo the
" price of money muft rife and fall to fit
                                      " their

" their occafions. We fee this by raifing
" the *exchange* at *Franckford*, and other
" places at the ufual times of their marts."

" The frequent and daily change in the
" low countries of their monies, is no fuch
" injuftice to any there as it would be here.
" For, being all either mechanics or mer-
" chants, they can rate accordingly their
" labours or their wares, whether it be coin
" or other merchandize, to the prefent con-
" dition of their own money in exchange."

" And our *Englifh* merchants, to whofe
" profeffion it properly belongs, do fo, ac-
" cording to the juft intrinfic value of their
" foreign coin, in all barter of commodi-
" ties, or exchange, except at ufance ;
" which we, that are ruled and tied by the
" extrinfic meafure of monies, in all our
" conftant reckonings and annual bargains
" at home, cannot do."

" And for us then to raife our coin at
" this time to equal their proportions, were
" but to render ourfelves to a perpetual in-
" certainty: for they will raife upon us
" daily then again ; which we of courfe
" fhould follow, elfe receive no profit by
" this prefent change ; we then deftroy the

C 4　　　" *policy*,

" *policy, juſtice, honour, and tranquillity* of
" our *ſtate* at home for ever."

I ſhall conclude this chapter with ſhewing :

10. *The ſeveral ways by which the ſtandard of money might be debaſed.*

What the ſtandard of money is, hath
been already fully ª explained : But to prevent miſtakes, I ſhall here recapitulate the
ſeveral ways by which this ſtandard may
be *debaſed, lowered,* or *curtailed* ; for all
theſe words here are ſynominous, and with
theſe, the phraſe *raiſing the money,* hath
alſo the ſame ſignification.

Firſt, By altering the denominations of the
coins, without making any alteration at the
mint, or in the coins themſelves ; as ſuppoſe
nine-pence, or as much ſilver as there is now
in nine-pence, ſhould be called a ſhilling ;
then a ſhilling would be called ſixteen-pence,
and ſo proportionably of all the other coins ;
and three crown pieces, or fifteen of our
preſent ſhillings, would be called a pound
ſterling, which is our money integer. The
ſame loſs would deſcend down to the penny,
and by this reckoning, the real penny muſt
be called $1\frac{1}{3}$ penny.

ª 31 &
32. I.

Or the alteration may be made at the mint, by either of the following methods.

Secondly, By continuing the fame names and the fame weights to the coins, but making them bafer, or with lefs filver and more alloy.

Thirdly, By preferving the fame finenefs of the metal, but making the coins fmaller or lighter.

Laftly, the two laft methods, or all the three methods, might be compounded together.

And here it may not be amifs to repeat again, that, by debafing the ftandard of money, I every where mean, the leffening of the quantity of pure filver in our *money integer* or *pound fterling,* or in the refpective fpecie which by law is ordained to make up that fum, without regarding the particular manner, in or by which, this may be done.

Each of the preceding fchemes for debafing the ftandard, have had their abettors. The firft of thefe was Mr. *Lowndes's* plan, and it muft be owned that this is by far the leaft mifchievous of them all ; for by this means a recoinage is avoided, and all the old coins are continued to be ufeful under

new

new names : but this is fo glaringly foolifh at firft fight, that our modern projectors do not think it would afford them any countenance.

Thofe who are for debafing the metal without leffening the weights of the coins, fay, that this would preferve the coin from wear : but this is faying either too much, or what is falfe; for were it true, the argument would bring us down to mere copper : But thofe who have been curious enough to make the experiment, know, that fine filver and fine gold, are lefs liable to wear than when alloyed.

The greateft number of the enemies to our ftandard, are to be ranged under the head of clippers, and perhaps this profitable trade is not quite out of their view ; they are for reducing the coins to a lefs fize, without altering the finenefs of the metal ; and with a grave air they fhamelefsly tell us, that this is not altering the ftandard of money,

C H A P-

CHAPTER II.

The established standard of money should not be violated or altered, under any pretence whatsoever.

T H E several citations in the foregoing chapter, are so full and direct to the point before us, that, one would almost think, the whole argument might be safely rested upon them. But notwithstanding all that hath been hitherto said, the subject is still misunderstood by many; and it must be confessed, that some points want to be better explained, than they have as yet been. For the better clearing it of all difficulties, I have in this chapter discussed the whole argument, independently of what hath been said by others ; and however that might be deemed to derogate from my own merit, I am the better pleased, the oftner I find myself in the company of those eminent authors already quoted. I have aimed throughout at brevity ; but the many attacks I had to encounter with, however frivolous they truly are, have unavoidably drawn this chapter into some length.

I. *Standards*

I. *Standards of all forts of meafures, necef-*
fary; and in the eftablifhment of thefe,
it is indifferent what are the fpecific quan-
tities or meafures taken.

11. In all regular governments or communities, it is very neceffary to have certain *ftandard meafures* eftablifhed, both as
to weight and extenfion ; that fo by thefe,
the true proportion between things as to
quantity, may be afcertained, and all dealings regulated with eafe and certainty ; and
it is very obvious, that a ftandard of money
is not lefs neceffary, than the others. Without thefe ftandards, moft bargains would
be vague and indeterminate ; and a door
would be left open for abufes, miftrufts,
endlefs ftrifes and controverfies.

It would have been of great conveniency
in reckonings, if all nations having mutual
intercourfes and commerce together, had
happened to have fixed and agreed upon
the fame ftandard meafures ; but in all
other refpects, this matter is quite indifferent:
Nor can it be faid, with any kind of propriety, that the ftandard meafures of any
one country, are either better or worfe than
thofe

thofe of another ; thofe meafures being either longer or fhorter, heavier or lighter, in
one place than they are in another, creating no manner of difference, when their refpective quantities and proportions to each
other are once known.   The *Flemifh* ell
and the *Englifh* yard, though differing con-
fiderably in lengths, are yet as good ftandard
meafures, one as the other. In like manner,
coins bearing the fame names, being made
either finer or heavier in one mint than
they are in another, create no manner of
difference in the cafe ; becaufe thefe coins
are every where rated accordingly.   Every
nation compares the meafures of all other
countries with its own ftandards; and no
advantage can enfue, by departing from thofe
already eftablifhed.

   12. This may fuffice as a full anfwer to
thofe, who are for debafing our ftandard,
becaufe fay they it is too good.   If our
crown piece is finer and heavier than a *Spa-
nifh* dollar, doth it not proportionably fetch
more ? or if it doth not, is there not fome
other caufe to be affigned for the difparity,
befides the quantity of metal in each ?
Thefe gentlemen might as well fay that our
yard is too long, and fhould be curtailed ;
and

and affign as a reafon for it, if they pleafe,
becaufe our confumption of cloth hath increafed, fince that ftandard was made and
placed in the exchequer: Or, that our bufhel
fhould be leffened, becaufe fome paft year
our crops of grain fell fhort. Of a piece
with thefe, when thoroughly fifted, will
appear moft of the reafons that have been
given for debafing the ftandard of money.

II. *Eftablifhed ftandards fhould be inviolably
kept, and more efpecially that of money.*

13. The ftandard meafures of a country
being once eftablifhed and known, any deviations from thefe afterwards could anfwer
no good purpofe; but, on the contrary,
they muft needs be attended with mifchievous confequences; they would difturb the
arithmetic of the country, confound fettled
ideas, create perplexities in dealings, and
fubject the ignorant and unwary to frauds
and abufes.

But of all ftandard meafures in any country, that of money is the moft important, and
what fhould be moft facredly kept, from
any violation or alteration whatfoever.   The
yard, the bufhel, the pound, *&c.* are applied only to particular commodities; and
fhould

fhould they be altered, the people would foon learn to accommodate themfelves in their bargains to the new meafures ; and it is but rare, that thefe have any retrofpect to preceding contracts. But money, is not only an univerfal meafure of the values of all things ; but is alfo at the fame time, the equivalent as well as the meafure, in all contracts, foreign as well as domeftic.

The laws have ordained, that coins having certain denominations, well known to every body, fhould contain certain affigned quantities of pure or fine filver. This makes our ftandard of money ; and the public faith is guaranty, that the mint fhall faithfully and ftrictly adhere to this ftandard. It is according to this ftandard, and under this folemn guaranty, that all our eftablifhments are fixed ; all our contracts, public and private, foreign and domeftic, are made and regulated.

Is it not felf-evident then, that no alteration can be made in the ftandard of money, without an opprobrious breach of the public faith with all the world ; without infringement of private property ; without falfifying of all precedent contracts ; without the rifque at leaft of producing infinite diforders, diftrufts and panics amongft ourfelves ; as all men would become thereby dubious

and

and infecure as to what might farther be
done hereafter ; without creating fufpicions
abroad, that there is fome canker in the
ftate ; without giving fuch a fhock to our
credit, as might not afterwards be eafily repaired ? Thefe wild and unjuftifiable meafures, have ever been and ever will be confidered, as a kind of public declaration of
fome inward debility and decay ; and the
difcredit occafioned thereby, has ever proved
injurious to thofe who ufed them.   All
payments abroad are regulated by the *courfe,*
of exchange, and that is founded upon the
intrinfic values, and not on the mere names
of coins.   But having once broke the public faith, and curtailed the fettled and long
eftablifhed meafure of property; foreigners
will make ample allowance for what we
may do of this kind hereafter ; and however we may cheat and rob one another,
they will not only fecure themfelves, but
make an advantage of our difcredit, by
bringing the exchange againft us beyond
the *par*.   If we think to avert this evil by
tranfporting our coin, our having debafed it
will avail us nothing.

III.

Why our laws are not more explicit in speci-
fying the quantities of silver that ought to
be contained in given sums of money.

14. As it is a matter of that very great
importance, to keep up inviolably the standard of money ; it may be asked, how comes
it that our laws are so silent in that respect,
as not to declare explicitly what that standard is, or what quantities of pure silver
ought to be contained in given sums of
money ; but rest satisfied, as it were, with
annexing their sanctions to mere names only ?

But the case is not so : For, although our
statute-books are silent, the indentures of
the mint are very express upon this head ;
and the forming of these indentures, hath
been always considered as part of the royal
prerogative. But it may be said with truth,
that this is a part of the prerogative that
never was, and never can be, exerted to
the altering of the standard, but with infinite detriment to the crown itself, as well
as to the subject. In former times, the
coins agreed exactly in quantities with the
common weights of the country, and had
the same names with them ; as pounds, shillings, and pence, were the names of the

D   com-

common weights, as well as thofe of fpecific coins and fums of money: At thofe
times, the bare names of coins and of given
fums of money, did manifeftly fpecify or
define the precife quantity of filver which
they ought to contain ; and then every one
could readily judge for himfelf, without the
affiftance of a law-book, and prevent any
fraud or impofition.   But although, by
the ftrange pranks that were afterwards
played in the dark fucceeding ages with
money, this bufinefs is now become fomewhat more obfcure; yet it is to be underftood, that our laws now mean, as well
as formerly, that fums of money under
certain names, fhall contain certain fpecific
quantities of filver ; otherwife their fanctions
are merely verbal, and in a matter of fuch
great importance, we are left in effect without any fecurity or law at all : But whatever
thofe of the long robe might determine upon the matter, the common fenfe of mankind hath determined in our favour ; and
the long refpite we have had, of above a
century and a half, from any abufes in the
ftandard of our money, hath given us a
kind of prefcriptive right, at leaft, to the
having of that ftandard kept unaltered.

There

There can be no fcheme fo weak or wicked, but there will be private men who will have, or fanfy they have, an intereft in pufhing it on; and when that is the cafe, we have too often feen all confiderations of public faith and private juftice, facrificed to the idol of private advantage. But any de-bafement, however fmall, of the ftandard of money, is fuch an outrage againft common fenfe, as well as common honefty, and fuch a manifeft violation of proper-ty; that it may be wondered how men having large poffeffions, and more efpe-cially minifters of ftate, could ever be brought to concur in meafures fo pernicious and deftructive to themfelves, to the public revenues, and to the public faith and credit. But although the ignorance of former times, fell into the fnares of wily projectors; it is to be hoped that in this enlightened age, we are fecure from being deceived into a fcheme, that would be attended with fuch infinite mifchiefs: And indeed in a reign remark-ably diftinguifhed by equal laws, and an equal diftribution of them; we need no other fecurity againft this enormous mea-fure, than the bare fhewing the enormity and injuftice of it.

III.

III. *The effects of debasing the standard of
money more particularly explained, and
who they are that would be the principal
sufferers by such a scheme.*

   15. *Trade requires an indelible standard
of money, and will bear no part of the
loss by an adulteration of the coins.*

[a] 53. I.   What hath been before [a] observed about
the invention of what they call *bank-money*,
in some of the neighbouring states, shews
very plainly, the folly and vanity, to give it
no harsher names, of adulterating coins;
it shews that trade requires, and will have
in effect, an indelible standard of money;
it shews that, do what you can, trade will
shift the burden off itself.   And as in those
places where *bank-money* is established, in con-
tradistinction to the current coin, the *aggio*
always rises whenever these coins are debased; so with us, where, (because the
standard having continued uniformly the
same, almost as long as we have been a trading nation,) no such distinction hath yet
obtained; if you alter the standard, the
tradesman will accordingly alter his reckoning, and raise the nominal prices of his
goods; or perhaps this wild measure would
                intro-

introduce amongft us, that aukward but neceffary contrivance of *bank-money* ; that is, a diftinction in dealings betwixt the old ftandard and the new ; and fo this fcheme would be defeated, though not without laying hardfhips on many, and creating general diforders and confufion. Or, if you fhould fuppofe that our tradefmen are fo fhort-fighted, and fuch bad accomptants, as not immediately to fee that 20, for example, is lefs than 21, foreign trade will foon open their eyes ; they will find that all forts of commodities will coft, at leaft, as much as they did before ; that is, they will be fold according to the old ftandard, or for fo much more according to the new reckoning, as the ftandard had been debafed. The courfe of exchanges would immediately fet this matter even ; the exchange will go yet farther, and take advantage of the difcredit, which ever accompanies thefe aukward and ill conditioned fchemes.

" But granting all this, fay you, all men " are not foreign dealers, and thofe tradef- " men who do not buy from abroad, will " have no pretence for raifing their commo- " dities."

In anfwer to this, I fay, that all men are in fome degree confumers of foreign com-

modities ;

modities ; and every one that hath the ſtaff
in his own hand will defend himſelf,
though he will give no further indulgence
to his neighbour, than what the law ſe-
cures to him. All tradeſmen are in ſome
ſort connected, and have mutual dealings
and dependencies one upon another ; and
foreign commodities enter deeply into all
branches of commerce. The neceſſary advancement in the nominal prices of ſo great
a part of our commodities, will naturally
affect the nominal prices of all the reſt ;
and were there no other reaſon for it, tradeſmen of all ſorts would endeavour to keep up
to the ſame proportion, one as the other :
And all ſorts of goods being thus once nominally raiſed, it would be difficult afterwards to bring them down to their old nominal prices, though the cauſe that raiſed
them be removed. But all the ſtock in
hand muſt be ſold at the former price,
that is, nominally at a higher, according as the ſtandard hath been debaſed ;
and goods even of our own manufacturing
could not be replaced, without paying nominally for them more than formerly. For,
the farmer finding all ſorts of goods he buys
in the ſhops, advanced upon him ; he will
alſo, though perhaps not immediately, raiſe

the

the prices of his corn, butter, cheefe, &c.
and fo the price of labour, and thence the
prices of all goods manufactured at home,
as well as thofe bought from abroad, muft
be nominally raifed, at leaft, proportionably
to the debafement of the ftandard.

Thus, I think, it is in a manner felf-evident, that a debafement of money, would
be fo far from laying any hold on tradefmen, that it would rather turn to their private advantage ; and therefore, in this debate, they are properly to be confidered as
being not very impartial advocates : Yet the
unavoidable difcredit and convulfions attending fuch a meafure, would prove injurious to trade in general, as well as to the
nation many ways. Let us next fee who
would be moftly affected, and how, by the
fcheme before us.

Debafing the ftandard of money, would prove
very injurious to the government.

16. If the money ftandard be curtailed,
fuppofe one twentieth part, and this by
many projectors would be reckoned a moderate alteration ; the king from thenceforward, would lofe a twentieth part of his
whole revenue. " Granted, fays our pro-
" jector ;

" jector ; but this will be no lofs to the
" crown, becaufe its difburfements will be
" alfo diminifhed a twentieth part." Not
fo, fay I : It is very evident, and I think abfolutely undeniable from what hath been
above fhewed, that all foreign ftores will
coft, at the leaft, as much as they did before, that is, they will coft nominally one
twentieth part more ; and not only thefe,
but likewife all forts of goods furnifhed by
our own tradefmen.   There will be then a
deficiency of, at the leaft, one twentieth,
in a very confiderable part of the public
difburfements.

How far thofe who receive falaries and
ftipends from the crown, might be com-
pelled to fubmit to this reduction, or how
far a reduction would in that cafe affect the
community, I do not take upon me to determine. But whilft many would be crufhed
by this indifcriminate fcheme, it is to be
feared too many others would make it a
handle for enlarging that dark, gnawing tax
upon their country, called by the delufive
name of * perquifites ; a tax, as well from
its enormous bulk, as from its indirect, oc-
cult, and undermining operations, though
                                                   lefs

* By perquifites, I do not here mean known and fettled
fees.   3

lefs perceived, perhaps infinitely more grievous to the public, than the whole lift of falaries in the court-calendar.

But admitting that perfons in civil offices,
might bear to have their falaries or ftipends
reduced; what would you do with thofe
upon the military eftablifhment, both land-
men and feamen? Is not their pay, officers
as well as private men, fcanty enough already? Or, could the officers quietly fubmit
to this reduction of their pay, and be kept
from clamour by good words inftead of
realities; what would you do with the common foldier and failor? Would you render
their ftate more abject and miferable than it
now is, was it in your power? But inftead of
their tamely fubmitting to thefe hardfhips,
you would put upon them; would you not
run the rifque of provoking a general mutiny? And how is all this diforder to be
rectified? No otherwife, than by raifing
nominally all taxes *5 per cent.* and fo raifing
murmurs, which though groundlefs, would
yet be loud. Try what methods you will
to deceive them, every one will fee and underftand that 19 is lefs than 20; and your
fcheme, after creating an univerfal difturb-
ance throughout the land, will, as to the
effect you prepofed by it, vanifh into fmoke.

De-

Debasing the standard of money would inva-
lidate all preceding contracts ; and yet, by its
affecting credit, might prove injurious to
debtors, and all in distressed circumstances.

17. As our laws do not directly specify
the quantities of silver that ought to be contained in certain coins and sums of money,
but annex their sanctions, as it were, to the
names only of coins ; should our coins be
legally debased, all contracts whatsoever
now subsisting among us, would be so far
vacated or annulled, as this debasement a-
mounted to ; every creditor would lose in
that proportion of his just right, and every
man of property might be greatly injured,
before he could have it in his power to
right himself. Supposing, as before, the
adulteration in the coin to be one twentieth
part ; the lawyers would stand to it, that
19 shillings, or so much silver as used to be
contained in 19 shillings, would be a full
discharge for a debt of a pound sterling ;
and so proportionably of all debts whatsoever.

There are a thousand cases, wherein creditors should shew compassion to their distressed debtors, and take such compositions
from

from them, as they are enabled to make.
But to make a kind of an univerſal compo-
ſition for debts, without any diſtinction of
caſes, is the ready way to the deſtruction
of all credit ; and ſuch a law, inſtead of
being advantageous to thoſe whom it would
ſeem to favour, might prove the very means
of their utter ruin: Their being diſengaged
from a part of their debt, would be but a
poor conſolation in the diſtreſſes they would
be likely to be thrown into, by their exaſ-
perated creditors.

*By debaſing the ſtandard of money, the greateſt
loſs would fall upon thoſe who live on their
own eſtabliſhed properties.*

18. It hath been already ſhewed, that,
ſhould the ſtandard of money be altered,
tradeſmen of all ſorts would help themſelves ; and they would probably ward off
ſome of the inconveniencies they would
otherwiſe be ſubject unto, by continuing to
reckon in the old money, which it is likely
they would call *old ſterling*. The deficiency
to the government muſt be made good, by
a nominal increaſe of taxes ; otherwiſe, ſome
of the wheels muſt ſtand ſtill. But all men
who live upon their own eſtates, or upon
eſtabliſhed ſtipends ; that is, all men who are

not

not fome how concerned in trade, would
have no way of helping themfelves, but
would be obliged to fubmit to the whole
lofs, which the law in this cafe would
throw upon them.   At the fame time, that
taxes, wages, and commodities of all forts
were raifed, at leaft, in proportion to the
debafement of the coin; rents, intereft of
money, *&c.* would be paid fhort of the original contracts; that is, they would be paid
and legally difcharged in the new money.
The landlord could not help himfelf, till
the leafes were expired; and the monied man
would be a lofer for ever, as he would
be † defrauded in both his principal and intereft.

Labourers and workmen of all forts,
would at firft be defrauded in their wages;
but this would not laft long; neceffity would
foon teach them to right themfelves; and
thofe that threw them under this neceffity,
would be anfwerable for all the tumults and
convulfions, which it might occafion.

Some

----

† And yet fome have been daring enough to ufe this
very fraud, as an argument for committing it : But of this
more hereafter.

*Some of the evils above enumerated, might
and ought be provided against ; but many
of them would remain irremediable, otherwise than by time, the great leveller of all
things.*

19. Some of the above evils might indeed, and undoubtedly fhould, be provided
againft, by enacting that all preceding contracts, fettlements and eftablifhments whatfoever, fhall remain good ; that is, that
they fhall be all fatisfied according to the
old ftandard. But this would be enacting
two laws deftructive of one another, at the
fame time ; creating new accounts to no fort
of purpofe, and involving all claffes of people in needlefs perplexities. And however
this laft act might repair our honour ; I am
afraid the two acts together, would not give
a very advantageous idea of our wifdom.
Whilft we were repairing one breach, and
the nations around ftaring at our folly, there
would be a thoufand inlets left for abufes ;
whilft the crafty evaded the laws, and made
their advantage of the confufion occafioned
by them; the ignorant and unwary would
be defrauded and diftreffed, and many of
them utterly ruined : Nor would it be in
the

the power of this healing act to allay, in a long time, the inevitable diftrufts, difcredit, murmurs and complaints, raifed by the other.

Debafing the ftandard of money, will occafion culling, and tranfporting of the old coins at an undervalue.

20. Trade is quick fighted, and no reftraint of law can hinder its purfuit of gain, wherever the game ftands fair ; and herein the uncircumcifed are juft as good markfmen, as the fons of circumcifion. In the prefent cafe, a temptation will be laid, and accordingly a new trade will be opened, for culling, and tranfporting all the good old coins, perhaps to purchafe others coined abroad in imitation of our new ftandard. Of the profits made by this new commerce, foreigners will have fome fhare, at our manifeft expence : In this refpect, trade is very generous, and readily divides fome of its fpoils on all fides. But you will fay, this evil may be prevented by opening the mint, and purchafing there all the old coins at their full value. And fo you will fave the nation harmlefs, at the moderate expence of a general recoinage : A wonderful expedient

dient truly ! But after the mint hath en-
groffed all the old coins, and whilft it is
coining the new; how will the internal
traffic of the country be carried on ? And
will not the diftreffes of the people, and
the uncertainties you have thrown them
into, by your new ftandard, be an invitation
to foreigners to coin and import upon you,
even worfe coins than you are a making at
your own mint. I am weary of the fubject; and it would be an endlefs purfuit to
go through all the inconveniencies, that
would attend this rueful project of debafing
the ftandard of money.

IV. *Caufes of debafing the ftandard of money,*
enquired into.

21. The mifchiefs occafioned by debafing
the ftandard of money, being fo glaring
and fo great; it may be afked, how was it
poffible that fuch a fcheme fhould be ever
entered into, and who could have an intereft in bringing it about ?

In dark times, weak princes and weak
counfellors, for fuch in this refpect they
were, might promife themfelves mighty
advantages from this device : They might
think to impofe upon the underftanding of
the

the fubject, and by this trick lengthen out
the ready cafh in the exchequer.   But they
did not, it feems, forefee, that this could
be only the fport of a day; that the whole
revenue would for the future be defrauded ;
that the deficiency could not be made good
without new impofts, which would create
murmurs, difcontents, and perhaps infur-
rections, amongft the people, *&c. &c.*

But I do not know how to think that
thefe fchemes really fprang from court,
however the courtiers might be bubbled into
them. There were others, whofe profpect
of gain by fuch a fcheme was much clearer
and better founded, and whofe influence
and credit in thefe matters, are ufually very
great ; as bankers, fcriveners, and all forts
of money-jobbers.   For by debafing the
ftandard of money, they were not only enabled to cheat all their creditors ; but alfo
furnifhed with opportunities of making large
gains, by taking advantages of the fears and
ignorance of the many ; buying up the old
coins at an undervalue, and culling and
tranfporting or fending into the mint all the
heavieft of them.

But nobody had fo clear and fo great an
intereft in thofe mifchievous projects, as the
                                        mint-

mint-mafters ; and it is to be fufpected,
that, by their credit and influence, they
had the greateft hand in bringing about the
feveral adulterations, that, time after time,
have been made in coins : They had an intereft in keeping the mint conftantly at
work ; and nothing could perpetuate this
gainful trade fo effectually, as adulterating
the ftandard of money ; this, in effect, reduced all the old coins into mere bullion,
and created an abfolute neceffity of a recoinage : By virtue of their places, thofe
gentlemen were fuppofed to be the moft
competent judges, and the moft to be re-
lied upon in thofe matters. If, befides theirs,
the opinions of the money-mongers were
afked, fuppofing they ftaid to be afked,
they would be fure to join with the mint;
and the feignorage formerly paid to the
crown for coinage, would be ufed as a
foothing argument for facilitating the project. By way of auxiliaries, there are at all
times troops of writers ready to be entertained, and ready to blow and propagate
any fcheme they are fet upon. When we
confider thefe circumftances, need we wonder if in former times, princes and their
minifters have been over-reached in this

E

bufinefs,

bufinefs, to their own very great lofs and
difgrace ?

V. *The various pretences for debafing the*
ftandard of money, ftated.

22. I imagine I have, in the preceding,
detected the caufes of the feveral adulterations that have been made in our coins;
but the real motives for this baneful meafure, were cloaked under various pretences;
and all that I have ever heard or read in its
fupport, I fhall under this head lay down
before the reader, and afterwards endeavour to anfwer all thefe affertions or pretences, feverally.

1. I have often heard it afferted, and that
by men who thought themfelves very wife
and knowing in thefe matters, that our
ftandard of money was too good, and fhould
be debafed. This ridiculous affertion hath
been anfwered b already; and nothing like
an argument can be urged in its fupport,
but what will fall under fome one of the following heads.

2. Increafing the coinage, and alfo increafing the quantity of tale money, by giving the old names to fmaller pieces of filver;

b 11, 12
& 13. II

are

are both urged as arguments for debafing the ftandard of money.

3. The keeping our coin from being melted or exported; alfo the examples of former times and of foreign ftates; are all brought as arguments for the fame purpofe.

4. The lightnefs of our coins from long wear, *&c.* is urged as an argument for altering the courfe of the mint, fo as to make the new coins no better than the old in common currency.

5. It is faid that debafing the coin, provided it be done gradually, a little at a time, would not be perceived, and therefore no injury to any body.

6. Some confine the ftandard to the finenefs only of the metal; and if that be but preferved, you may clip or diminifh the coins as you pleafe.

Thefe are all common-place thread-bare arguments, ready upon all occafions; and founded only upon this fuppofition, that as good money may be coined at the ftamp-office, as at the mint: But our modern projectors have found out new arguments, and, as they think, very formidable ones.

7. Some fay that gold is our ftandard as much as filver; and therefore that no argu-

ment

ment can be ufed as to the one, but will
hold equally with refpect to the other.

8. Others go yet farther ; and fay that
gold only is our ftandard ; that you may
debafe filver coins as you pleafe, and treat
them as mere tokens, without giving any
one a right to complain. This is making
fhort work of it indeed, and with one ftroke
demolifhing our poor old ftandard : And in
fupport of this it is faid, that gold is the
ftandard of merchants ; and therefore is, or
ought to be, the national ftandard.

There is an obvious neceffity of bringing
the rates of gold and filver coins, to a jufter
proportion to each other, than they bear
at prefent ; and as fomething fhould be
fpeedily done, it is faid in favour of gold,

9. That, as we have greater plenty of gold
coins, and of far greater value than we
have of filver ; fhould we lower the price
of gold, we fhould undervalue our own
treafure ; therefore fay they curtail the filver
ftandard.

10. Some more modeft than the reft,
are for debafing fome of our coins only, as
fhillings and fix-pences : And leaving the
crowns and half-crowns upon their prefent
footing ; they think that would be fufficient

to

to fecure them, from the odium of having debafed the ftandard.

Laftly, As we are a nation indebted to foreigners; fhould we lower the price of gold, we fhould pay our foreign creditors more than we borrowed from them; therefore we fhould debafe the filver, &c.

This is very artfully put, and hath really in it more of argument, than all the preceding put together. But the whole weight of that argument, lies upon a fraud couched under it; a fraud that could not well be avowed, and yet would be glaring and obvious to all the world.

Before I enter upon the merits of thefe feveral pretences, for debafing the ftandard of our money; I fhall endeavour to remove an obftacle out of the way, which, I believe, hath proved a ftumbling block to many well meaning people.

VI. *Why coin and bullion of the fame metal and finenefs, are not always of the fame value, or will not exchange in equal quantities one for the other.*

23. Silver and gold with us, are meafured by the ounce troy; and the legal rate of an ounce of either of thefe metals in coin, is

Mint price what.

called the *mint price*; that is, filver being the ftandard, and the coinage with us being free ; the number of pence that an ounce troy of ftandard filver is cut into, is called, though perhaps improperly, the mint price of filver ; and the number of pounds, fhillings and pence, with fuch a fraction as may happen, that falls to the fhare of the ounce troy of gold, according to the legal rates of guineas, is called the mint-price of gold. Thus, becaufe 62 fhillings are cut out of a pound troy of filver; 62 pence, or 5 *s.* 2 *d.* is faid to be the *mint price of filver :* And 44½ guineas being, by the indentures of the mint, cut out of a pound troy of gold, and guineas now paffing at the rate of 21 fhillings ; this makes the prefent *mint price of gold* with us, to be 3 *l.* 17 *s.* 10½ the ounce. In both cafes, the finenefs is underftood to be according to the eftablifhed ftandard ; *viz.* the filver to be 11 *oz.* 2 *dwts* fine, and the gold 11 *oz.* or 22 *car.* fine.

If the importers of bullion into the mint, pay a certain rate for the coinage, as in other countries ; the rate which they pay is to be deducted from the mint-price above ftated, and the refidue is then the mint price. *Ex. gr.* If the importers of
bullion

bullion into the mint paid, fuppofe, two-
pence an ounce for coining filver ; the mint
price of filver bullion, would be then five
fhillings an ounce ; and at this rate it would
frequently be in our market, if no other
caufe interfered.

Bullion can never be lower, but may fre-
quently be higher, than mint price.

24. Whether the coinage be free or otherwife, if the mint be always * ready to make
its returns in coin ; neither filver nor gold
bullion, can fall in our market below mint
price; for the mint is always open to receive them both, at thofe refpective rates :
But one or both thefe metals, may be frequently higher than mint price.

1. If the bullion is exportable by law,
and the coin is not, without fome penalty ;
this, whenever we want to make any confiderable remittances abroad, may fomewhat
advance the price of bullion ; and that in
proportion to the demand for, or fcarcity of,
bullion.   But the advanced price of bul-
E 4   lion,

---

* This is a neceffary condition ; for a delay here might
oblige the merchant to fell his bullion at an undervalue, to
thofe who could better ftay to have it coined.

lion, on account of the mere inexportability
of coins, I think, muſt be very inconſider-
able ; as coins may be reduced into bullion,
at a ſmall riſk of diſcovery, and at a ſmall
expence. For, the demand for bullion upon
this account, is chiefly in great towns, where
the melting-pot is always at work; and it
is very eaſy to conceal the contents, from the
knowledge of any ſervant or by-ſtander.

2. Although both coins and bullion were
legally exportable ; yet the market price of
bullion, might be frequently above the mint
price. For, the remitter might not have by
him, or be able readily to procure, a ſufficient quantity of * weighty coins to anſwer his preſent purpoſe ; in that caſe, he
will not ſcruple giving ſome advanced price
for bullion; and he will be reimburſed with
profit, by thoſe who want his bills upon
that place, to which the bullion is to be
ſent † : Or, if he himſelf be the debtor
abroad, he may find it cheaper to give an
advanced price for bullion, than the pur-
chaſing of bills of exchange. But upon the
preſent ſuppoſition alſo, of coin being exportable ;

* For all coins in foreign dominions are mere bullion,
and treated as ſuch.

† See more upon this head, in the firſt part of this Eſſay,
chap. III.

portable; the advanced price of bullion cannot be confiderable or permanent, unlefs there be fome other caufe co-operating.

3. If the coins pafs by tale, and are by wear or otherwife become fenfibly lighter than their juft ftandard, at their firft coming out of the mint; this, when there is a demand for exportation, will naturally raife bullion above mint price. But the difference between coin and bullion upon this account, cannot exceed the average of the whole deficiency upon the coins; and it will fall fomething fhort of that average, becaufe the heavieft coins will be firft fent abroad; and by being fent, keep down the price of bullion : And when the demand for exportation is fatisfied, bullion will again fall to mint-price.

4. If the current coins are heavy, or pafs by weight, and the merchants or importers of bullion into the mint, pay a certain rate for coinage, as the cafe is in all other countries; bullion at times, will fall as much below coin, as this rate amounts to; that is, a given quantity of bullion, might be purchafed for fo much lefs quantity of coin, as the coinage of that bullion would coft at the mint.

Thefe

These different causes may concur, to vary a little the price of bullion; and to raise it, sometimes more and sometimes less, above mint-price, as exigencies vary; whilst it can never be lower than that price: But the effects of these causes are only temporary, and never very considerable.

5. The arrival of plate fleets from *America*, and the departure or fitting out of fleets for the *East-Indies*; have, perhaps, greater influence upon the market price of bullion, than all the preceding causes put together: But because those incidents upon the arrival and departure of the said ships, are irregular, and usually of short continuance; no great stress need be laid upon them in this place.

Some of the causes, above enumerated, of the disparity between coin and bullion, occurred to Mr. *Locke*; but, having missed of the principal cause for his purpose, which here comes next to be considered; he brought himself under some embarassments, by laying a greater stress upon the others, than they were able to support.

VII.

VII. *If gold and silver coins are not rated in*
due proportion to each other, as they are
at a medium in the neighbouring countries ;
that metal in bullion, which is lowest rated,
will raise and keep constantly above mint-
price, till that cause be removed.

25. It hath been shewed in the preceding, that coin and bullion will not always
exchange in equal quantities one for the
other, although we had only one sort of
coins, as silver, for instance, in currency;
and the case would not be very different,
though we had both silver and gold coins,
if the legal rates of these were established
in a due proportion, as they are at a medium in the neighbouring countries. For,
bullion being a commodity, its price will
fluctuate a little, so as sometimes to be above
coin ; and it hath been shewed, that it can
never be lower than mint price. But the
difference upon the above accounts, can
only be at particular times, and then not
very considerable.

Silver bullion in England hath been for
above half a century past, constantly higher
than mint price, excepting only at a very
few intervals of a short continuance. This

hath

owing to gold being higher rated at our
mint in proportion to ſilver, than it is in
other countries : For, the cauſes conſidered
in the preceding, affect equally both gold
and ſilver; and their influence upon both,
may be deduced from the ſhare they have
had upon gold. For, gold only coming into
our mint, the deviations of gold bullion
from mint-price, ſhew, accurately enough,
the effects of the ſeveral concurring cauſes
before-mentioned, upon the price of bullion
both gold and ſilver; and they ſhew alſo,
that theſe effects are but ſmall, and uſually
of no long continuance.

To illuſtrate the caſe before us : Let us
ſuppoſe that in *England*, gold coins are rated
* five *per cent.* higher in proportion to
ſilver ; or if you would rather conſider it
ſo, that ſilver coins are rated ſo much lower
in proportion to gold, than in the neighbouring countries. This ſuppoſed diſparity
of five *per cent.* is three-pence upon a
crown-piece, and about a ſhilling upon a
guinea ; that is, gold coins with us are
rated a ſhilling in the pound ſterling too
high;

* I do not take upon me, in this place, to ſtate how
much it is that we over-rate gold ; the exact proportion between gold and ſilver, not affecting the preſent argument.

high ; or, which is the fame thing, filver coins are rated a fhilling in the pound fterling too low, in refpect to guineas. But the law reaching only to coins, and bullion being free ; the market will adjuft the difproportion which the law had made ; and either, filver bullion will rife above coin, or gold bullion will fall below the rate of guineas ; till, as abovefaid, the legal difproportion between gold and filver is adjufted. But no bullion can fall below the rate of coin, whatever that rate be ; the mint being always ready to exchange coin for bullion, at the legal or mint-price. Therefore the difference, in the prefent cafe of filver being loweft rated, will fall entirely upon the filver ; that is, whilft the mint becomes a ftandard for the price of gold bullion, filver will rife in our market the above fuppofed difference of five *per cent.* or to about 65 pence the ounce, or to five fhillings and three-pence, for as much filver as there is in a crown-piece. For, the merchant will always make that metal his ftandard, which is higheft valued at the mint ; and, in the prefent cafe, he will not part with his filver at a lefs rate in proportion to gold, than it will fetch him in other countries.

Both
2

Both gold and filver in the eye of com‑
merce, are commodities; and that equally,
whether they be in the fhape of coins or
bullion ; and the market prices of both with
refpect to one another, will be nearly the
fame every where, without regarding the
mint prices in different places. Gold, as
above inftanced, being higheft rated with
us, will be brought here in great plenty ;
efpecially, whilft any heavy filver coins are
to be had in exchange for it : But no filver
can be brought in here, or worked into
plate, till the market price of it hath rofe,
fo as to make it equally profitable to import
either filver bullion or gold; and filver
being excluded from our mint, by the
higher valuation there of gold, no more
filver can ftay here, than what is wrought
into plate. For, a guinea fetching here as
much of any thing, as can be purchafed for
21 fhillings ; and in *Holland*, fuppofe,
fetching no more than may be purchafed
with 20 of the fame fhillings ; a merchant
here will not part with a filver ingot, at a
lefs rate than that of a guinea for 20 fhil‑
lings : If the refiner or filverfmith will not
give him at that rate ; he will fend his ingot
to *Holland*, and there purchafe with it, either
gold, a bill of exchange, or fome other com‑
modity,

modity, that will fetch him here as much
as the money he had aſked for the ſaid ingot;
all charges being paid, which are pretty
nearly equal, for the tranſportation of both
gold and ſilver.

Trade is too quick-ſighted to be over-
reached by laws; and gold and ſilver bullion are too univerſally known and coveted,
to ſuffer any diſparity in reſpect of one another : The *European* markets are never
glutted with either, and they will fetch proportionably every where. Gold then being
over-rated at our mint, ſilver bullion will
get up as much above coin, as this over-
rate amounts to; and, in like manner,
ſhould gold coins be undervalued, gold bullion would riſe as ſilver had done before.
Theſe metals have every where a reference
one to the other; and without this, the
terms higher or lower rated, could have had
no place.

VIII. *Difference betwixt money and mere*
bullion, farther illuſtrated.

26. Foreign commerce, as hath been before obſerved, treats gold and ſilver as commodities, both alike; and they are ſubject
to fluctuate in their value, not only with
                                  reſpect

respect to one another, but also with respect to all other commodities, according to their greater plenty or scarcity. But nevertheless, in all home establishments and transactions whatsoever, one of these metals is money, or a standard measure of the values of all other things ; and this standard cannot be altered, without incurring all the mischiefs before enumerated.

As bullion occurs much more than coin, in the transactions of merchants ; some of them have been induced from thence to think, that the price of bullion is what governs and measures, the values of all other things. But, from what hath been already delivered, it is very manifest, that the price of bullion is governed as well as measured, by coin or the established standard of money ; and not suffered to deviate much, from that standard. With merchants indeed, any commodity they deal in, may be said indifferently to be a standard for all the rest, as well as gold or silver ; for they consider all things, as they will purchase more or less of each the other, in this place or in that ; and coins, which with the rest of the world is money, is with them thrown into the general hotch-potch, and no otherwise distinguished

guiſhed from other commodities, but from the proportion that certain quantities of one or the other, will fetch of the reſt ; and they join with us rather in language than in idea, as to the uſe of coins. No wonder then, if theſe gentlemen treat the ſtandard of money ſo ſlightly, and ſo diſdainfully, as ſome of them do. But although we are all agreed, that gold and ſilver, like all other things, have their values increaſed or depreciated, according as they grow ſcarcer or in greater plenty ; and that the coins made of them, do, in this ſenſe, ſhare the ſame fate with the bullion : Yet coins as ſuch, or as money, eſcape the fluctuations of markets ; and the ſtandard coins, which are the meaſures of all contracts, are to be conſidered as having their value remaining permanent and unalterable ; the above ſlow alteration brought about by time in the value of money, being not to be admitted into conſideration, in the temporary dealings of men with one another.

Having thus explained, as clearly as I could, the ſeveral cauſes of the different prices of coin and bullion ; the eſſential differences there is between them ; and alſo the effect which the over-rating of gold hath upon ſilver bullion : Let us now proceed to

F   conſider,

confider, the feveral pretences that are urged
for debafing the ftandard of money.

IX. *Coinages fhould in no wife be forced.*

27. The keeping of the mint perpetually
at work, feems to be the main drift of all
the common maxims about coins; and the
feeding of this office, is profeffedly urged
as one of the reafons, for debafing the
ftandard of money : And it muft be owned
indeed, that nothing could be more effectual
for the compaffing of that end.   But this is
propofing one evil, as a reafon for committing
another.   The evils attending a general recoinage, which this fcheme would inevitably bring about, are many and great; but
without entering into a detail of thefe evils
at prefent; let it here fuffice, to examine
into the merits of that notion, which is very
generally entertained, that coinages are by
all means to be encouraged.

In one fenfe, coining is a neutral, harmlefs, and indifferent act; for if it be left free,
it neither inriches nor impoverifhes the nation, one fingle penny; the coins juft pay
for the bullion whereof they were made,
and the profits to the mint are fpent a-
mongft ourfelves.   But it deferves well to be
con-

confidered, that coining is neverthelefs an
act of very great importance : That a very
great truft is thereby lodged in the mint ;
that it requires very great care, and great
fkill too, in thofe intrufted, to keep exactly
to the ftandard ; that a fmall deviation from
it upon each piece, would foon amount
to a large fum ; that coins are univerfal
pledges ; and that the credit of nations is
greatly concerned, in the exactnefs and faith-
fulnefs of their mints.   When thefe things
are confidered, will it follow that coinages
are to be promoted unneceffarily ?   That
coins once faithfully made of their due finenefs, are to be melted into the unattefted
ftate of bullion, for no other purpofe than
to be recoined again ?

*Purchafing bullion at an advanced rate for coin-
ing, a very weak and infignificant meafure.*

28. Befides debafing the ftandard, another expedient hath been hit upon for feeding the mint ; and that is, the purchafing
of bullion at an advanced price for coining,
or the giving more *per* ounce for the bullion, than it would be afterwards worth in
coin.   But although this meafure is very
harmlefs, as to any confequence attending
it,   excepting to thofe immediately con-

cerned ;

cerned; yet it cannot be reckoned a very
wife one. For, whatever be the caufe that
prevents bullion from coming into the mint;
whilft that caufe fubfifts, and coining will not
remove it, the new coins will be melted into bullion again, and again coined ; and fo
round in a circle, as long as a *præmium* to
the importer of bullion into the mint, is
continued. And after all this expence, and
all the expectation raifed from it, no new
coins will be to be feen; the fame caufe
that created a fcarcity before, will carry all
thefe away; and nothing will be left, but the
gains that had been made at the mint.

After what hath been faid here, and in
the preceding ; it might be afked, of what
ufe then is the mint ? To which I anfwer,
that a mint, rightly eftablifhed, is a very
ufeful, neceffary, and important office ; an
office, that thofe at the head of our finances
fhould have due cognizance of, as being
anfwerable to the public, that its operations
are faithfully performed. The natural wafte
and diffipation of coins, require frequent
fupplies : This, trade naturally and abundantly furnifhes ; and this vent for its bullion, when other markets do not invite, is
alfo of very great advantage to trade ; it
prevents a ftagnation and uncertainty, in a
very

very confiderable branch of commerce. No
mint can be kept conftantly at work, unlefs coining becomes a kind of manufactury
for foreign commerce; which is not the
cafe here, nor could it be, without very
great lofs to us, upon our prefent mint eftablifhment.   But the mint, if left free to its
own natural courfe, cannot fail of keeping
up the national coins to their due quantity;
what it does more, may be truly faid to be
labour loft; and would prove mifchievous, if trade did not ftep in and fweep away
the fuperfluous coin.

What hath been here faid, regards coining
in general; without refpecting the difpa-
ragements, which either filver or gold coins
may lie under in particular, at the mint;
and it may ferve as a full anfwer to thofe,
who are for promoting coinages, by forced
and unnatural methods.

X. *Curtailing the ftandard will not lengthen
out the coin; but, on the contrary, will
occafion a greater fcarcity in common currency.*

29. Some fay, that if the ftandard of money was curtailed, the quantity of money in
tale would be thereby proportionably in-
F 3   creafed;

creafed; which they think would be a notable
benefit to the country : As if the ftandard
was curtailed a tenth part, we fhould immediately have a tenth part more money, than
we had the moment before.   According to
this maxim, we have a very fhort and eafy
method of becoming rich; for if it holds
in any one proportion, as here a tenth part,
it will hold in any other; and whilft we are
about it, why not take off a good piece,
and leave only fuppofe one hundredth part
behind ? By this expedient, with one million
of the old money, we could not only pay off
all our old debts; but have enough left for
carrying on the war, at leaft for a year or
two longer ; and all this, without raifing one
penny of taxes upon the fubject.   A very
fine device truly !

ᵇ 50. I.   I have already ᵇ fhewed that all artificial
methods of increafing tale-money, are, fo far
as they extend, pernicious.   But the fcheme
before us, will not reach the end propofed by
it : If the method be by calling a fhilling,
fuppofe, thirteen pence; although this would
be attended with the mifchiefs before enumerated ; yet, in the common traffic of the
country, a fhilling, notwithftanding the law,
would be called a fhilling ftill ; and fetch and
go, juft at the fame rate as it did before. If
                                                 you

you give us new coins debafed according to the new ftandard, this will rather make the matter worfe. All things will advance in their nominal prices, at leaft, proportionably to the debafement made in the ftandard : This is a point wherein the underftandings of men, cannot be impofed upon by mere founds ; fo that were all the old coins new minted, they would go not one jot the farther, than they would before this alteration. But, from the alarms, fears, and fufpicions, which this woeful project would naturally raife in the minds of the people ; many of the coins would be hoarded, and many tranfported : So that the mint would be left gaping with little to do, and the country diftreffed for want of coin. All this, I think, upon even a flight view of the cafe, muft needs appear very evident ; but I do not wifh to fee it confirmed, by fo pernicious an experiment.

XI. *Debafing the ftandard, would not prevent coins from being melted, or exported.*

30. There are many well-meaning people, who think it the intereft of their country, to keep the national coins from going abroad ; and that this end might be accomplifhed, by debafing the ftandard of

F 4   money.

money. I fhall not at prefent enter into the merits of this conceit of keeping our cafh at home ; nor inquire what influence fuch a fcheme, if it could be effected, would have upon our commerce and credit ; but I think that a very flight reflection is fufficient to con- vince any one, that the means propofed would not anfwer the end. An adulteration of our coin cannot remove or affect any one of thofe caufes, whatever thofe may be, that bring foreign demands upon us for money : Thefe demands muft be fatisfied, to the full weight of fine filver or fine gold. Fo- reigners will not be impofed upon by names, or by falfe meafures ; if our coins are adul- terated, by being made either bafer or lighter, they muft have more of them ; and probably even fomewhat more than their due, from the unavoidable difcredit attending any debafement of money. Fo- reign coins are every where treated as mere bullion ; and fhould we debafe ours, as much pure filver or pure gold, at leaft, would be carried abroad in thefe new coins, as now go- eth in thofe of the prefent ftandard. Our own coins indeed, becaufe of the free coin- age, are in effect even at home, as much bul- lion as whilft they were in the mafs ; and the

the ftamp of itfelf, is too weak to fave them from the melting pot.

If the proportion between gold and filver coins, was brought and kept to a juft par; this would prevent either of thefe coins from being melted or exported, preferable to the other; but it would not leffen the exportation upon the whole, excepting fo far as coins made of one of thefe metals, as filver for inftance, might be fent abroad to purchafe gold for coining. This is an evil we have laboured under, and the remedy is obvious, without medling with the ftandard of money.

XII. *Foreign ftates debafing their coins, is not a reafon for the debafing of ours.*

31. Some people are fo fond of the projeçt of tampering with the ftandard of money, that any thing will ferve them as a plea for that purpofe ; and, I think, nothing can well be poorer than the following, which yet I have heard urged with fome vehemence, *viz.* " that certain foreign " ftates having debafed their coins, we " fhould therefore debafe ours." This empty plea, for it cannot be called an argument, hath been fpoken to, in the preceding

chap-

* chapter.   It might, in truth, as well be
faid, that we ought to change our language, as change our ftandard; the plea
here brought for the one, being equally
concluſive for the other.

^c 41. I,   It hath been before ^c ſhewed, that it is
out of the power of laws directly, either to
augment or diminiſh the values of coins in
general, otherwiſe than as by their oblique
influence, they may increaſe or diminiſh the
whole quantity of them in circulation.   But
ſtates may ſet a higher value upon one
fort of coins, in proportion to others, than
is done by their neighbours; as we have
done by gold coins in reſpect to ſilver:
The conſequence of which, always hath
been, and always will be, the draining
away of the coins that are undervalued.
States may, if they pleaſe, go yet farther,
and ſet a higher value upon ſome ſpecie of
coins, than they do upon others made of
the ſame metal; and the conſequence will
be as before, the draining away of thoſe
that are leaſt valued, and leaving them always poorer upon the whole; for the coins
that are undervalued, will always go away
at ſome undervalue.   But of this more hereafter.

There

* Page 22, 23.

'There are, perhaps, no greater inftances of human weaknefs, than the various and contradictory meafures that have been purfued, almoft all the world over, about coins. And even, in the fame country, oppofite meafures have been taken, without any difference of circumftance to occafion them : But, an opinion it feems prevailed, that, fince one method had not the defired effect, the contrary muft needs fucceed ; and this again failing, fome new courfe was again taken, and fo on. The effects of all the various tamperings that have been made with coins, have ever proved, and ever will prove, that no alteration can be made in the ftandard of money, but what will be injurious many ways to thofe who make it ; and it may be prefumed, that no argument can be brought for that wild meafure, either from what hath been done here or elfewhere, but what will conclude ftrongly on the other fide of the queftion.

XIII. *The lightnefs of our coins, not a reafon for altering the ftandard.*

32. It is well known that a great part of our current coins, what by long wear, and what by fraudulent practices, are become much lighter than the legal ftandard.

Some

Some argue from hence, " that the ſtand-
" ard itſelf ſhould be leſſened accordingly ;
" and ſay, that this would be doing no in-
" jury to individuals, if the new coins be
" made no worſe, than the generality of
" thoſe that are now in common currency."

This is an old plea, and which in any
other caſe but that of money, would appear
ſufficiently ridiculous to every body : To
diminiſh the ſtandard upon this motive,
would be ſuch a vague purſuit as could
have no end ; and what would, in effect,
leave us without any ſtandard. If this argument had been admitted ; our ſtandard,
and our coins, would ere now have been
in a manner annihilated ; and in trying to
follow after them, the price of a ſhoulder
of mutton would now be reckoned at as
many millions, as would pay off the whole
national debt in our preſent coin.

But this ſcheme, upon the plan propoſed,
is in fact impracticable : What particular
piece or bag of light coins, is to be taken
for the new ſtandard ? And when this is
fixed upon, what is to be done with the
other coins, that are either heavier or lighter
than theſe ? Are the weighty coins to
be clipped, and the light ones to be new
minted to the new ſtandard ? Who does

not fee the abfurdity and evil confequences
of fuch a fcheme ? Should the meafures in
common ufe, fome by wear and fome by
fraudulent diminutions, become many of
them lefs than the ftandards at the exchequer; and it were propofed to diminifh
thofe ftandards accordingly; would not fuch
propofal be manifeftly very ridiculous ? And
are not the cafes nearly parallel of money,
and other meafures ? Or, doth not what difference there is, turn entirely on the fide of
the money ftandard, as money is both an
equivalent and a meafure ?

The effects of diminifhing coins by law, and
what they fuffer in private hands, very
different. Currency by tale, regards chiefly
the ftandard, or original value at the mint.

33. The confequences of what the coins
fuffer in private hands, are widely different
from thofe that would follow their debafement by legal authority. In the one cafe,
every man's right is left unviolated ; for
he may refufe coins unlawfully diminifhed,
if he pleafes; and he hath no body to
blame but himfelf, if he doth not : And
as for thofe coins that are become light
by long wear ; fo long as all forts of coins,
light and heavy, continue indifcriminately

to

to exchange one for the other; the damage from the lightnefs of coins, doth
not, as yet, fall upon individuals.   But
fhould the coins be debafed by authority,
every man's property would be invaded ;
all forts of goods would rife, at leaft, to
the new ftandard ; and all the evil confequences before enumerated, would inevitably follow.

It is to be obferved, that in the currency
of coins by tale, no regard at all is had to
their lightnefs, or deficiencies arifing from
mere wear ; but all pafs, as if they were of
their due ftandard or full weight, as they
firft came out of the mint.   All fixed eftablifhments, being really made and governed
by the legal ftandard ; have a great influence, efpecially that of the public revenue,
in keeping up the current values of coins
towards that ftandard, notwithftanding their
diminutions by long wear.   And although
foreign commerce contributes its fhare,
towards bringing the current values of
coins, nearer to the real value ; yet, as the
coins that go abroad, and they only are to
be confidered in the prefent argument, bear
but a fmall proportion to thofe paffing in
all our internal tranfactions ; their effect in
account-

accounting for the lightnefs of our coins, muft needs be very inconfiderable.

The above obfervations cut off at once all pretences for debafing the ftandard, from the lightnefs of the current coins; fince that lightnefs, is in no wife confidered, in any of our internal dealings with one another. Currency by tale refers only to the legal ftandard, as currency by weight doth to the coins themfelves; and there is this farther notable difference between them; that by the one, the coins are perpetually kept up to the real ftandard, or fo as to pafs only for their real value; whilft by the other, the deficiency upon the coins is fo much dead lofs to the public; which lofs muft, fooner or later, reach to individuals, however they may ward it off for the prefent.

To conclude this head, let us put a cafe the moft favourable poffible to our opponents in the prefent argument: Suppofe that all our coins were equally deficient in value, according to their refpective current rates, as one twentieth part; and it were to be declared by legal authority, that the coins, as they now ftand, are of the due ftandard. This declaration, would cut off one twentieth part of every man's property, though all contracts would continue to be

2   dif-

difcharged and paid, in the very fame coins
that they were, before this new declaration.
The plea of not having debafed the ftandard, below the value of the actual coins in
common currency, would be no juftification
of this meafure; and with refpect to the
alienation of property, this proceeding would
have the very fame effect, as if all the current coins were now of their full weight,
according to the prefent ftandard, and were
called in to be diminifhed one twentieth
part; whether by clipping, or new minting,
would alter not the cafe.

XIV. *Any infringement of the ftandard of*
money, however fmall, would be proportion-
ably injurious.

34. There are fome who readily allow,
that a great debafement of the ftandard at
once, would be very injurious ; " and yet
" infift, that if you do it gently, a little at
" a time, no harm will be done; they fay,
" fuch a gentle touch would not be per-
" ceived, and therefore none would com-
" plain."
Strange indeed! You fay it would be
injurious to debafe the ftandard much at
once, and yet that it would be no injury to
                                             do

do the fame thing at feveral times. But
ftrange as this logic may feem to be, it
muft be owned to be very ingenuous, and
to afford perhaps as good an argument for
the purpofe, as any we have yet met with :
It fairly owns that debafing the ftandard
would be a fraud, and only aims at fhewing how you might commit this fraud without being perceived. It would be in vain
to argue with thefe gentlemen upon moral
principles ; but here we can anfwer them
upon their own : The law muft be pro-
mulged, before fuch a project could be executed ; and by that previous notice, the
whole defign would be fruftrated.

XV. *All the fpecies of coins made of the
fame metal, fhould be rated in a juft proportion to each other.*

35. There are fome who readily agree,
that the debafing of all our coins would be
attended with evil confequences ; and yet
think, that " thefe evils might be averted,
" and the ftandard fufficiently fecured, by
" the largeft fpecie of our coins only, as
" crowns and half-crowns ; whilft the lower
" fpecie, as fix-pences and fhillings might
" be debafed ; and the debafing of thefe
" they think would be advantageous, as it
G   " would

" would be a means of preventing their
" exportation, and of keeping them en-
" tirely at home for our own circulation."

I shall say nothing here to the notion of
keeping our coins from being *exported; and
it hath been shewed ª elsewhere, that there
cannot be a want of coins for home circulation, unless † substitutes be placed in their
stead : In that case, indeed, there may be
frequently a want of coins for the circulating of the substitutes ; and the only effectual way of curing the evil, is by gradually
destroying those substitutes.   Remove the
cause, and the effect will cease.   But the
notion of having two sorts of coin, one pas-
sing for more than it is worth, or at a greater
rate than the other, is a most dangerous
one ;   and could it be brought to effect,
would not only be injurious according to
the proportion of value, which the sum
total of these base coins may bear to all the
rest ; but also be attended with another fatal
consequence peculiar to itself ; the draining us of all our good specie.   The mint
                                                        at

ª 49 &
50. I.

---

* This notion, which is a very general one, I fansy was
first broached and propagated by the bankers ; they might
think, if the quantity of circulating cash could be increased,
it would be brought the faster into their shops, and be suffered to stay there the longer before it was again recalled.

† Gold, copper, or paper-money, may either jointly or
separately, be the means of draining away silver coins.

at the *Tower*, would foon be eafed of its labour of making thefe bafe coins; and not only private hands amongft ourfelves, would have a fhare. in this beneficial trade; but foreigners alfo would not let flip fo fair an occafion of minting, and importing upon us thefe bafe coins, fo long as we had any good ones to give them in exchange. For example, if you were to coin fhillings, having in them only nine penny-worth of filver; fo long as a crown-piece could be had for five of thefe bafe fhillings, you might be fure that plenty of them would be coined, both at *Birmingham* and abroad. This confequence is natural; and every nation ought to guard carefully, that all its feveral fpecie of coins, be rated in their due and juft proportion; otherwife, thofe that are higheft rated, muft needs in time drain and fwallow up all the reft.

But it is not probable that fuch a fcheme, if it was attempted, could with us be brought to effect; and yet it might be attended with fuch perplexities in all dealings and contracts, both home and foreign, as for a long time back we have been free from in this country: It is moft likely, that in all future contracts, it would be diftinguifhed in what fort of money the contracts were made, and

the

the bargains regulated accordingly ; for it
is to be hoped that all preceding contracts,
would be left to be satisfied in the old money : Or, the people would take and pass
the new coins for their real worth ; and in
either case, the whole scheme would be
frustrated. As supposing the new six-pence
should be worth the old groat ; the people
would either reckon in the different proportions of two and three in all their dealings, according as they contracted in old or
new money : Or, to avoid this perplexity,
they would call the new six-pence, a groat ;
and fifteen of them would as currently exchange for a crown-piece, as ten old ones
do at present.

XVI. *Silver only, and not gold, is the stand-*
ard of our money ; and not the less so, be-
cause gold coins have a fixed rate by law.

34, 35,   36. It hath been before ᵇ shewed, that
36, & 37   there can be but one standard of money ;
Ĩ   that in these parts of the world, silver is,
and time immemorial hath been, the mo-
ney standard ; and that it is the fittest material, hitherto known, for a standard.

We never heard till lately, a word mentioned of gold being the standard of money :

ney: Former projectors saw the abfurdity of
calling any thing the ftandard, befides that
by which all the accounts of the country
were kept, and all contracts meafured. But
their fucceffors are grown defperate ; and
fuch is their fondnefs for gold, that any
thing will ferve them as a plea both for
debafing filver, and for making gold the
ftandard ; at leaft, they would have it bear
a fhare jointly with filver : And, for this,
gold coins having a ftated price by law, they
think is a fufficient argument.   However
this fact, at firft fight, might miflead fome
people ; yet, it is very certain, that the argument built upon it, is overthrown by the
very words of the law itfelf.   Is not a declaration that a guinea fhall pafs for twenty-
one fhillings, a plain reference to fhillings,
as a ftandard meafure of the value of a guinea ? But, it cannot be faid, on the other
fide, that a guinea is a meafure of the value
of fhillings ; it is impoffible that any whole,
fhould be made up of the parts of a material different from itfelf. The laws, the language of the country, the common confent, and common fenfe of all men, have
unanimoufly concurred in making filver
our only ftandard. Every body knows that
pounds, fhillings, and pence, denote cer-
G 3   tain

tain fpecific quantities of pure filver ; and whilft all contracts whatfoever are meafured by thefe, it would be a ftrange perverfion of language, to call any thing elfe the ftandard. My receiving a certain number of guineas, in confideration for a certain fum, or number of pounds fterling, doth not make gold money, or a ftandard ; any more than if I had received to the fame value in lead, wheat, cloth, &c. would thefe commodities have thereby become money. Gold being coined, alters not the cafe ; the coining only afcertains the quantity of metal, contained in the feveral pieces, at their utterance out of the mint ; and we have proper meafures at hand, for determining the quantities of other commodities. There is a neceffity of coining gold to afcertain its finenefs; otherwife, it would be a commodity too precarious to be meddled with in common dealings ; a difference of finenefs imperceptible to the eye, making a very great one in the real value.

But you will fay, that gold coins, excepting the difference of colour, and of fome other properties of the metals, have as much the appearance of money as filver coins : Granted ; and fo have copper coins
too ;

too; and so might pewter ones, *&c.* but
this is nothing to the purpose; it is not the
mint, but the laws, and the universal con-
currence of mankind, that make money.
You will say again, that the laws oblige me
to take gold, as, or instead of money;
whereas, I am at liberty to refuse any other
commodity, that may be offered me instead of money.   True; and I have be-
fore shewed * the propriety and conveniency   * 38.I.
of ordaining that gold coins, should pass at
certain rates, *pro tempore*, as or instead of
money?   But still, this doth not make gold
money : These rates are not to be fixed
arbitrarily, but are to be regulated by the
price which gold then bears, in respect to
silver as a standard ; and these rates are,
and always have been, considered as being
subject to this rule ; and so to be altered
again and again, whenever the case may so
require.   Under this limitation, it is very
convenient, that gold coins should pass as
or instead of money, but not as being themselves money, or the standard measure of the
values of all other things.   It is a fundamental characteristic of money, that, as a measure,
it continues invariable ; that is, that a payment in the standard coins, of any specific

fum or quantity of money agreed upon, is, whenever made, a full difcharge of that contract; without regarding at all, how filver may have varied in its value with refpect to commodities in general, by an increafe or decreafe of its quantity. But gold coins are to be confidered in another view : Payments in them, may not be by quantity for quantity; it is by the rates only, which gold coins bear in refpect to filver as a ftandard, at the time of payment, that contracts are difcharged ; and not according to the rates, which thefe coins might have, at the time when the contracts were made. In this view only, gold coins are to be confidered ; and, in this view, they are upon a footing with any other commodity; though lefs liable to a fudden and great change in their value, than moft other things.

Much of the difficulty upon this fubject hath arofe, from the not attending to the difference between money and commodity ; and again, by confounding with the ftandard the lightnefs of the coins paffing by tale, and making every coin, as it were, to be itfelf a ftandard. But this is bringing into the argument, what the common fenfe and common practice of men, never thought of.   The nature and condition of tale money

ney hath been already ² explained ; and, ² 33. II.
I think, it is fufficiently manifeft, that all
contracts and the prices of commodities,
are meafured by the ftandard, and not by
the intrinfic value of coins, in countries
where they pafs by tale : Nor, where they
both pafs promifcuoufly, is there any difference in regard to payments made either
in gold or filver coins ; in all cafes, the filver ftandard is alike the meafure referred
to.   I do not here enter into the merits
of paffing coins by tale ; I have only aimed
at fhewing what it is that conftitutes tale-
money.   But gold coins, although they
paffed only by weight, would fo far partake
of the nature of tale money, as not to have
the prices of things, *&c.* regulated by their
rates or intrinfic value ; but only, as above
obferved, by the eftablifhed filver ftandard.

XVII. *Gold being made the ftandard by mer-*
chants, doth not make gold to be the national
ftandard.

37. It hath been before ᵇ obferved, that ᵇ 58. I.
merchants will reckon by that metal which
is moft common in large payments ; all
coins are with them, in effect, mere bullion ; they have no regard to names, or lo-
                                                        cal

cal inftitutions; the real quantity of pure
filver or pure gold, which they give and
take in exchange for other commodities, is
what they reckon by. And it is very manifeft, by the courfe of exchange between
us and all the world, that gold here is the
ftandard of merchants; and this for them is
moft profitable, becaufe gold here goes far-
theft in the purchafe of our commodities;
but with what lofs to the nation, doth not
fall within our prefent confideration.

But the tranfactions of * merchants, do
not make a ftandard for the reft of the
world; and indeed, as hath been before
obferved, they have in effect no money, as
they do not confider it in the fame light
that others do; coins with them being mere
merchandife, as much as cloth, iron, or
any other commodity. And therefore no
confiderations from the practices of merchants, or from the courfe of exchanges,
have abfolutely any thing to do in the prefent debate. In all countries, the bufinefs
of fettling the ftandard of money, is purely

a

---

* I confider merchants here and elfewhere, folely as foreign dealers, without regarding their private tranfactions
with fhop keepers, &c. in the places where they dwell;
in this laft light. they are upon the fame footing with all
other private dealers.

a national concern, which the reft of the world have nothing to do with ; and merchants, as fuch, are of no country. If you alter the ftandard, whatever effect it may have among yourfelves, the courfe of exchange will fet the matter even as to the reft of the world. If you lower the price of gold, the exchange in appearance will turn proportionably in your favour ; if you debafe your filver ftandard, it will go feemingly againft you, to the full amount of this debafement: That is, in both cafes, the exchange will really fet the matter even ; and therefore, as above obferved, the confideration of exchanges hath nothing to do in the prefent argument.

The great inland commerce or bufinefs of this country, is chiefly carried on, fcarce as it is, by filver. Labourers, handy-craftfmen, and manufacturers of all forts, are paid their day wages in filver : What they receive is palpably, and manifeftly their ftandard ; and as labour is the main foundation of all riches, what goes to pay the price of it, will be the real ftandard of the nation, even though laws were enacted to the contrary. Laws, though they may, and perhaps too often do, perplex, yet they can-

not

not eradicate fettled ideas. Workmen of all forts here, have fixed ideas annexed to fhillings ; they do not know, perhaps, the precife quantity of filver which they ought to contain ; yet they know that there is an old eftablifhed law, that hath fettled this matter : Whilft this law is not abrogated or tampered with, they think themfelves fafe ; they are content with their ufual wages, without fcrutinizing into the precife quantity of filver in the refpective coins ; whilft the fame laws fubfift, they expect thefe coins will fetch them as much neceffaries as ufual, and they look no farther. You may raife or lower the price of guineas, as the cafe may require, without affecting the price of labour ; and therefore without affecting the price of any home commodity, in the firft inftance.

It hath been obferved before, and the thing is fufficiently manifeft, that the ideas of filver are annexed to pounds and fhillings ; and no law can transfer thofe ideas to gold, or to any thing elfe. The farmer underftands that he hath contracted to pay a certain number of pounds fterling for rent : This rent may be fatisfied or difcharged with gold, barley, horfes, &c. thefe commodities refpectively, being fuppofed at

the

the time to be worth fo much filver, or fo
many pounds and fhillings, as they reckon
for. And what reafon is there for fixing
the idea of ftandard, to any one of thefe
commodities, preferably to the reft ? The
fame reafoning may be extended to all other
things ; for all things may, and often do,
anfwer the purpofe of money ; but yet this
doth not make commodities to be money,
nor money a commodity. The rent is
equally difcharged with gold or barley, according to the refpective rates, which certain quantities of thefe commodities have at
the time of payment. Nor does the more
uniform and certain quality of the one, make
any difference in the prefent argument ; it
preferves indeed the price of a given quantity, at a more equable rate ; but it is fubject neverthelefs to have that price altered,
as the great market of the world may go-
vern ; and for fuch an alteration, no one
can have juft caufe to complain : But the
cafe is very different with refpect to filver.

Thus, I think, it is very manifeft that
filver, and only filver, is the ftandard of the
country, of all contracts and eftablifhments
there, whatever may be the ftandard at the
Royal-Exchange : And, I think, that it would
be impoffible at prefent, to transfer the
ftandard

ſtandard from ſilver to gold. Enact what
laws you pleaſe ; what meaſures and pays
the price of labour, will be ultimately the
real ſtandard of the nation ; and gold is at
preſent too dear for the payment of day wages,
and for the purchaſe of ſmall neceſſaries.
Enough hath been ſaid before, to ſhew the
iniquity of altering the ſtandard of money ;
and, I think, that enough alſo hath been
ſaid, to ſhew the vanity and folly of ſuch
an attempt. But to inſtance again, only in
the caſe of labour : If ſhillings be debaſed,
ſuppoſe a fifth, or any other given part, either by changing their uſual rate of 12 pence,
or the $\frac{1}{20}$ of a pound ſterling, or by putting
leſs ſilver in them ; the workman will ſoon
underſtand, that he muſt have the part
lopped off made good to him, by increaſing
his nominal wages. This matter is ſo obvious, that he cannot be impoſed upon, and
the very attempt of doing it, might be attended with fatal conſequences.

XVIII.

XVIII. *Lowering the price of gold would be of no loſs to the nation ; and the lowering it directly, by leſſening its rate* per *ounce or* per *guinea, would be of leſs loſs to individuals, than if the ſame was done indirectly, by debaſing the ſtandard, or leſſening the quantity of ſilver in the pound ſterling.*

38. It is, in effect, agreed on all ſides, that the price of gold ſhould be reduced; but for debaſing the ſtandard, or as they call it, raiſing the value of ſilver, it is ſaid : " That " as our ſtock is chiefly in gold, ſhould we " depreciate or leſſen the rates of guineas, " it would be undervaluing our own trea- " ſure, and bringing a great loſs both upon " the nation and upon individuals; but, as we " have a ſcarcity of ſilver coins, the debaſ- " ing of theſe would be ſo little felt, as not " to be worth regarding."

We have already met with many pretences for debaſing the ſtandard ; which, upon examination, appeared ſufficiently weak and frivolous : But amongſt them all, I think, there is not one quite ſo vague and ridiculous, as this before us. Let us ſuppoſe that the reduction, wanted to be made in

2   the

the rate of a guinea, is one shilling; for it is nothing to the argument, what the precise quantity really is; and that will come to be considered in another place. You say, that if the rate of a guinea be reduced one shilling, there would be a loss of the one and twentieth part, upon all the guineas in the nation; but that there would be no loss at all upon guineas, if they were ordered to pass for twenty one shillings, having in them no more silver, than there is at present in twenty shillings. Strange, very strange indeed, that there should be such magic in the word shilling, and in the number twenty-one, as to make the same thing, only calling it by different names, have such different effects! It is scarce necessary to take any farther notice of such a mere jingle of words; but out of tenderness to these young logicians, but more out of regard to those who may be deceived by them, if any such there can be: I shall endeavour to shew, that our scheme is more favourable to them, than their own.

1. It is self evident, that the nation would not lose one farthing upon all the gold it exported, by a reduction of the mint price of gold. For this reduction, would not in the least debase the intrinsic quality of the gold;

gold ; and every guinea that went into foreign parts, would fetch there as much afterwards, as it doth at prefent ; unlefs, perhaps, there is now a trade abroad for purchafing guineas, and re-exporting them to
us again'; and, if there be fuch a trade, it
is much to our difadvantage.

2. Let us fuppofe, that the reduction is
made, by calling twenty of our prefent fhillings, by the name of twenty-one fhillings ;
or, which is the fame thing, by a new coinage wherein twenty-one pieces, called fhillings, are cut out of the fame quantity of
filver, as before ufed to be put into twenty
fhillings. Here, it is felf-evident, that every
one will lofe a fhilling upon a guinea ; and that
his lofs will be in the fame proportion, upon
all the filver coins which he hath to receive.
For, it hath been fhewed, that the prices of
all things at home, are regulated by the filver
ftandard ; and therefore they would foon raife
againft us, in proportion as that ftandard
had been debafed ; unlefs you think, that
founding the words *twenty-one* in their ears,
would lull men afleep, and deprive them of
their underftanding. By this fcheme then,
the one and twentieth part of all their cafh,
gold as well as filver, would be taken away

from, and irrecoverably loft to, every body ;
and this lofs would fall, not only upon the
prefent ftock in hand, but alfo upon all that
they had to receive for the future, in confideration of any contracts already made.

3. Let us fuppofe, that the rate of a guinea is, without ufing any other indirect
means, directly reduced to twenty * fhillings. Here then, whilft his property in
general is left † unviolated, both now and
in future ; the only lofs any one can fuftain,
is upon his prefent ftock in hand of guineas, and this lofs cannot exceed one fhilling upon each. But, it is not improbable,
that by the falling of commodities, there
might be fome abatement of this lofs :
For, by the conceffions of thofe who abett
the contrary meafure, they making gold
to be the ftandard of merchants, foreign
exchanges will alter in our favour, proportionably to our reduction upon gold ;
and with the exchanges, it is likely, the
prices

---

* The conceit of a late writer, of reducing the price of
guineas by a general recoinage of them into a larger fize,
and his arguments drawn from the inconveniencies that
would thence arife, require no anfwer.

† It hath been clearly fhewed in divers parts of this effay,
that the rates of gold coins are, from their very inftitution,
fubject to alteration ; and the making of this alteration as
often as the cafe may require, is in all refpects juft, prudent,
and neceffary.

prices of all foreign commodities, would
in some degree likewise alter, which would
also cause an abatement in the prices of our
own.

It is difficult to state to any exactness,
what influence foreign exchanges or the dealings of merchants, have upon the prices of
goods in general ; that is, how far our high
valuation of gold, and so the mercantile
trade, may clash with the legal standard, in
measuring the values of contracts and of
commodities : I admit, that this may have
some effect ; but, I think, for the reasons
which have been already given, that this
effect is very inconsiderable.

But to bring this whole debate, as far as
it any way relates to our present subject, to
a short issue : If it be admitted that contracts, and the prices of all things, are governed wholly by the established silver standard ; then, it is manifest, that if you alter
that standard, the prices of all things will
raise, at least, in that proportion : On the
other hand, if you insist that gold is the
standard ; then, I say, that if you lower its
price, and that will be equally done by
either of the preceding methods, the prices
of all things will fall proportionably. But

whether gold hath any fhare jointly with
filver, in fettling and meafuring the prices
of things; or, whether gold takes all upon
itfelf; it is as clear as the day, that, according to which method is taken in adjufting
the prefent difproportion between the legal
rates of gold and filver, there will follow a
difference, at leaft, in the prices of things
in general, to the full amount of that difproportion : And, it is as clear, that our
method of reducing them, would be by
much the moft favourable to the prefent
poffeffors of guineas, as well as a fecurity to
them of their full property for the future;
which, by the other method, would be invaded and taken from them, to the whole
amount of the reduction or debafement of
the ftandard.   But is there need of balan-
cing, fo exactly, the immediate profits and
lofs, between thefe two different methods,
of reducing the price of gold? The one, all
the world knows, is fair, equitable, and perfectly agreeable to public faith ; whilft the
other, would be reproachful, unjuft, and a
thoufand ways injurious, both to the ftate
and to individuals. The cafe of men as they
are mere debtors and creditors, hath been
already confidered; and fo far as they are
equally fo, it hath nothing to do with the
                                              prefent

prefent argument; and we fhall have again
occafion to fpeak more to this point a little
farther on. In its proper place, the cafes of
bankers, and public receivers, fhall be duly
confidered.

XIX. *The nation being in debt to foreigners,*
is not a reafon for altering the ftandard.

39. I am now come in the laft place, to
confider a pretence for debafing the ftandard
of money, on which much ftrefs is laid
by fome perfons, *viz.*

" As we are a nation indebted to fo-
" reigners, have great plenty of gold coins,
" and no filver coins but what are much
" below the ftandard ; fhould we lower
" gold, we fhould undervalue our own trea-
" fure, and pay our foreign creditors more
" than we received from them; and no in-
" juftice would be done, fhould we make
" gold the ftandard, and raife the filver."

In this argument, many different things
are artfully blended together, that the main
defign of cheating our foreign creditors
might appear the lefs confpicuous, and the
lefs fhocking. All the above various pretences have already, in effect, been fully
anfwered ; but becaufe of the importance

H 3   of

of the fubject, I fhall here fpeak again to
fome of thefe points.

1. If the intention be fimply to transfer
the ftandard from filver to gold, why are
the filver coins to be altered? Doth not the
altering of them, equally alter the fize of
the ftandard, commit equally the fame injuftice with refpect to property, whether
you call the new ftandard by the name of
gold, or by the name of filver? And hath
all the pother made about gold being a
ftandard, any other aim or defign, than to
deceive us by a mere jingle of words? Or,
is it poffible, that any can be fo hood-
winked as to believe themfelves, that gold
either is or ever can be the ftandard, whilft
it continues to be fo dear, and whilft all
men do and continue to reckon by filver?

2. It is a fact too notorious, that we have
no filver coins left, but what are wore much
below the ftandard; and that even thefe are at
length grown fo fcarce, as to call aloud for
a fpeedy fupply. But one part of the argument grafted upon this misfortune, *viz.*
" that by lowering directly the price of gold,
" we fhould undervalue our own treafure,"
hath been fully anfwered in the preceding;
and there it hath been alfo fhewed, that the
lowering of gold directly or openly, would
be

be eafier or lefs detrimental to individuals, than
the doing it, as it were covertly, and clan-
deftinely, by debafing the filver ftandard;
and enough hath been already ᵃ faid, to fhew ᵃ 11 to 20
the vanity, injuftice, and enormity of fuch   II.
a meafure. Thofe alfo, who would perfuade
us that in reality and practice, gold is our
ftandard, becaufe with us more payments,
or to a much greater value, are made in gold
than in filver coins; have been likewife, I
think, fully ᵇ anfwered. And I might go ᵇ 36, 37
yet farther, and infift, that although our   II.
filver coins were grown yet fcarcer, or were
even annihilated; as long as filver continued
to be plenty in tne reft of the world, and as
long as we continued our old method of
reckoning in pounds fterling; thofe old abo-
lifhed coins would continue ftill to be our
ftandard; and their fubftitutes, whether they
be gold, copper, or whatever elfe, would
have their value according to that proportion, which given quantities of them bore
to the quantity of filver formerly put into
thofe old coins, into whofe places they had
fucceeded. Nothing could be really the
ftandard, but that which all men called the
ftandard; and there could be no other way
of eftimating the value of the fubftitute, than
by the value of the thing to which it was

H 4   referred.

referred. Settled ideas, annexed to the names
of known things, are not to be eradicated,
or even altered, whilst the things themfelves continue unaltered.   If circumstances
did fo require, which is not the case at prefent, nor likely to be fo in ages yet to come,
the standard of money might be transferred,
from filver to fome other material ; but, to
make this transfer complete and effectual,
it would be neceffary to lay afide the old
names ufed in reckonings and accounts, and
to fubftitute new ones in their ftead : To
transfer the ftandard of money from one material to another, was the thing itself proper
and requifite, is not fo eafy to be accomplifhed, as fome late projectors feem to
imagine.   But to proceed.

Former tranfactions have no relation to the
prefent value of money.

^a 21 I.   40. It hath been before ^a fhewed, that
money is a ftandard meafure by its quantity
only, without regarding in the leaft the
fluctuating value of its material with refpect to other things. This reftriction to
quantity only, is effential to the nature and
very being of money, as without which it
would lofe its place as fuch, and dwindle
into

into mere commodity : How could that be called money, the value or price of which was fluctuating ; and at all markets, and in all contracts to be bargained for, like other commodities ? But should we admit money to be a commodity ; those who would infer from thence, that the standard of money should be debased, are very unlucky in the choice of their argument, for it proves directly against them ; as it is notorious that in *Europe*, both gold and silver have been gradually, and, I might say, continually sinking in their value for a long time past, from the continual increase of their quantity : And upon this principle, the standard of money should be inlarged, and not curtailed ; and all creditors, both public and private, would have an undoubted right to demand back a greater quantity, than they had lent.   But how could the several claims be adjusted, according to the different times of the respective loans ? What infinite contests, distractions and confusions, must needs follow any departure from the true nature and use of money ?

It hath been also abundantly proved, both in this and the preceding part of this essay, that silver only and not gold, is, and time immemorial hath been, the measure of all

our

our contracts : And therefore the inference
in the preceding, *viz.* " As we have great
" plenty of gold coins, fhould we lower
" the price of gold we fhould undervalue
" our own treafure, and pay our foreign
" creditors more than we received from
" them ;" this inference, I fay, is falla-
cious, and nothing to the purpofe. But before I proceed any farther, I cannot help
taking notice of the artifice ufed, in making
the application to our *foreign* creditors *only* :
How could this diftinction be fupported in
practice ; and if it could, where would be
the juftice of it, and what would become
of the public faith? Was not that faith
given, or which is the fame thing, underftood to be given, to all forts of creditors
indifcriminately, that they fhould be paid
again by the fame fcale that the loans were
meafured with? And was this fcale anything
elfe than fterling money, or our prefent filver ftandard?

    That affertion, that lowering the price of
gold would be undervaluing our own trea-
sure, hath been before fufficiently   anfwered : And almoft every part of this
whole chapter, is a full anfwer to the application above made to our public creditors ;
and indeed, creditors of all forts would be
the

ª 38 II.

the greateft of fufferers by a debafement of
money, as their loffes would be irretrievable
and paft all redemption.   But to fpeak more
particularly to the point before us : Admitting, what is hardly to be admitted, that all
our loans have been made in gold coins;
and that thefe coins at the feveral times of
borrowing, were, as at prefent they manifeftly are, over-rated : This over-rating of
gold was undoubtedly prejudicial to us ; and
this prejudice we fhall continue to fuftain, till
the caufe is removed.   But this hath nothing
to do in the prefent debate : The fcale by
which we borrowed, was filver; and it muft
have been underftood, that we engaged to
pay by the fame fcale, whenever the day of
payment came.   The due proportion of value of gold to filver, or the juft rates which
gold coins ought then to have, was not confidered by either fide ; nothing was regarded
but the current rates, at which on the one
fide they were given, and on the other taken,
in full confideration of certain fpecific quantities of filver; which filver, was on both
fides underftood to be, and for ever to continue to be, the true and only meafure of
the contracts.

Again, our loans were made for prefent
ufe ; and the money, in the fame fpecie, and

2   at

at the fame rates, as we received it; was, foon after the borrowing, difperfed into other channels, for fuch things, fervices, and confiderations, as were then deemed an equivalent. And by thefe difperfions, the public efcap'd the immediate lofs from receiving gold at too high a rate. But in truth, our over-rating gold, is a confideration to be referred wholly elfewhere; and from which, nothing can be fairly drawn that may affect the prefent argument.

Every true patriot wifhes to fee our public debt reduced; and grievous as the burden at prefent is, there is great room to hope, that the time is not far off, when our expences may be leffened, and our debts gradually difcharged, in a manner that fhall be confiftent with the faith, honour and renown of the nation; and of this we need not defpair, if the wife, juft, and folid maxims of our prefent adminiftrators, will be imitated and followed by their fucceffors. But whatever may be the fate of future times, and whatever the exigencies of affairs may require; it is to be wifhed that that aukward, clandeftine, and moft direful method of cancelling debts, by debafing the ftandard of money, will be the laft that fhall be
thought

thought of ; as that method would make a havock alike of all property, and create universal panics and distrusts, not easily to be afterwards repaired.

XX. *Of debasing, or raising the nominal values of, coins in general.*

41. We have now gone through the several pretences, that have been urged for debasing the standard of money; and they were chiefly founded upon the disproportion between the rates of gold and silver coins with us, in respect to what they bear at a medium, in the neighbouring countries: But there are some so extravagant, and so lost to all common sense, who not content with debasing the standard coins only, would have us debase both gold and silver at the same time; and they are so precise as to tell us, to a grain, how much per ounce they would debase both the one and the other: But as these grave computists, do not offer us any reasons in support of their notion; mine is, that they be left to themselves to compute on, as they please.

By the proclamations, &c. cited in the preceding chapter, the mischiefs that had been occasioned here by adulterating the

3   coins

coins in some former reigns, appear very
manifest. Besides the infinite confusion,
distrusts, and panics, created by those measures throughout the realm ; they were ineffectual as to the end proposed by them :
The people would part neither with their
old money, nor their goods, according to the
new standard ; and having lost their old
scale, were forced upon the primitive method of trucking one commodity against
another. *France* affords us a more recent
instance, of the bad effects of these measures ; these are plainly set forth by an ingenious *French* author, in a book entitled,
*Political reflections upon the finances and
commerce of France* *. This piece enters
necessarily too much into a detail of those
bad effects, to have any part of it inserted
here ; it fully answers and confutes, by
plain and undeniable matters of fact, another *French* piece, wrote professedly in justi-
fication of the adulterations, that had been
made at different times in the *French* coins.

But notwithstanding that both experience
and the reason of the thing, are so evidently
and strongly on our side, against all tamperings

---

* This piece is translated into *English*, and was printed
for *A. Miller* in the *Strand*, anno 1739.

ings with money; yet, is .there but little profpect of quite filencing the contrary doctrine. I was not a little furprifed to fee it infinuated, in * a work containing many excellent obfervations relative to trade, that the profperity of *France*, was greatly owing to the pranks that had been played with coins, by *Lewis* XIV. I do not know whether I fhould have taken notice of the above paffages, if the fame doctrine was not now again revived, and delivered in much plainer terms by Mr. *Poftlethwayt*, in his late work entitled, *Britain's commercial intereft explained and improved*, vol. II. page 354. I have no doubt of this laborious gentieman's good intention; but as the doctrine infinuated in the paffage referred to, is fo directly contrary to all that I have been inculcating, it would be unfair not to lay it before the reader, at full length.

" LABOUR in France is but 3 *d.* per day
" of 14 hours, or from five to feven o'clock,
" in the cheapeft countries, and about 7 *d.*
" half-penny in the deareft: in manufac-
" tures, at but half the price as in England.
" Sailors wages a-board the French navy, but
                                        from

* * *

* *Britifh Merchant*, vol. I. p. 6, 7, 10, 16, 17. Small Edition.

" from 8 to 12*s.* per month; whereas in Eng-
" land, a failor has 20*s.* per month a-board
" king's fhips. Muft not this render their
" commodities exceeding cheap in compa-
" rifon to ours at foreign markets?

" A N D here it may be obferved, that
" this cheapnefs of labour, provifions, and
" commodities, was, at firft brought about
" by the fole artifice of the enhancement of
" their money from 27 livres, to 50 livres
" the mark of eight ounces of filver troy-
" weight; and this has been done fince the
" beginning of the confederate war in 1702.
" It is true, this caufed great convulfions in
" the kingdom at firft, but in the iffue, it
" has been the inftrument by which they
" have fapped the foundations of our trade;
" and, if a remedy be not applied, this arti-
" fice of the French will worm out Britifh
" manufactures by gentle degrees in every
" market in the world: and that no lefs in
" time of war than peace, by virtue of neu-
" tral powers carrying on their trade for
" them; which they cannot do to fuch ad-
" vantage by Britifh commodities, by reafon
" of their greater dearnefs.

" By this artifice they have rendered their
" labour fo cheap, that they reap a plenti-
" ful harveft in every country, *where they*
" *pay*

" *pay but the same customs as the English,*
" whilst the English merchant is obliged
" to wait for the gleanings of the market,
" after the Frenchman has finished his
" sales.

" THE project of the enhancement of
" money, has given an undue preference
" in France to money, above land and
" commodities : but where lies the disad-
" vantage at present, if the gentleman re-
" ceives but a hundred pound weight of
" silver for his lands, where he used to re-
" ceive two hundred pound, if, at the same
" time, he can purchase as many commo-
" dities with a hundred pound, as before
" the enhancement he could with two? It
" is certain it would only affect his foreign
" consumption. By this scheme the French
" have restrained the bulk of the people to
" the consumption of their own manufac-
" tures, and commodities, and have pro-
" digiously extended their commerce, by
" underselling all nations. This has enabled
" their islands to send home sugars, indico,
" &c. so cheap, as to rival us in all the
" European markets, and in the Levant:
" and all this they do, though their manu-
" factures pay six times as much in taxes
" on the necessaries of life as they do in
" England.

I   " DUTOT

" Dutot fays, the price of bread, corn,
" and provifions, is no greater now than in
" 1683 ; though in this laft year the mark
" of filver was but 27 livres *, and now
" 50 are coined out of it. This circum-
" ftance, as obferved, has rendered their
" commodities fo cheap, that they under-
" fell us, and engrofs all the markets in
" the world from our merchants. It is
" likewife this enhancement of their coin,
" and the confequent cheapnefs of their
" commodities, which has enabled our
" fmugglers to carry on fuch an advan-
" tageous trade with them. If but 20 *l.*
" 5 *s.* were now coined out of their mark
" of filver of eight ounces troy weight,
" which was the cafe in the year, 1660,
" the French would not be able to fell a
" gallon of brandy under 5 *s.* fterling,
" which now they can fell for 2 *s.* ; nor a
" pound of tea under 7 *s.* 6 *d.* fterling,
" which they now fell for 3 fhillings ; nor
" a yard of filk damafk under 12 *s.* 6 *d.*
" which they now fell for 5 fhillings ; nor
" a yard of cloth under 15 *s.* which they
" now fell for 6 fhillings, abating only in
" the manufactures, the difference made in
                                    " the

" * When the mark was at 20 livres about 1660, labour
" was dearer in France than in England."

" the price of thofe manufactures, with re-
" gard to the raw-materials, which coft
" both French and Englifh men much the
" fame, though the raw filk comes to them
" cheaper from the Turkey-traders; and
" their wool ufed in their fine woollen
" ftuffs dearer from our fmugglers than
" to us." A little farther on Mr. *P.* feems
to lament our cafe, becaufe, " Our confti-
" tution and public faith will not admit us
" to play fuch tricks with our money as the
" French have done."

The whole of this gloomy tedious tale,
is fo marvelous and vifionary; that were it
not fo gravely and circumftantially told, one
could fcarce have believed the author to be
really in earneft. It would be needlefs here
to enter into particulars; but from the
whole, I think, it clearly follows, that if
the cafe was as it is above ftated, our condition would be, as Mr. *P.* feems to dread,
a moft deplorable one indeed. We fhould
be every hour at the mercy of our enemies,
as by the fimple artifice only of fplitting their
coins into halves, they might, as by a magic
wand, at once double their force againft us;
and if that would not be fufficient to crufh
and utterly deftroy us, they need but keep
fplitting on, till at length their coin be anni-

hilated,

hilated, and by that fimple expedient, obtain
that univerfal dominion, which it is faid they
have been fo long in queft of.

But from their adherence to the fame
ftandard of money, for fo many years back,
it feems that the *French* have quite another
notion of this bufinefs; it feems as if they
had opened their eyes at laft, and feen, from
woeful experience, the folly and mifchief of
debafing the ftandard of money; and whatever reception this debafing doctrine may
meet with at *London*, it is very probable
that at *Paris*, it would be treated with that
contempt and indignation, which it fo well
deferves.   Mr. *P.* laments nothing fo much
as the greatnefs of day-wages in *England*;
but there feems to be no other natural remedy for this evil, than a general poverty;
and we have politicians, that, could they
but once get at the helm, would foon
bring this about; and perhaps the debafing
of money would be as effectual for the purpofe, as any one fcheme that could be
thought of.   But from the poor, tattered
and ftarved condition in general, of the commonalty of *France*, it feems very evident
that there, the lownefs of wages, of foldiers
pay, *&c.* is forced and not natural.   De-
fpotic power can do this; can draw to itfelf

felf what fhare it pleafes of every one's property, and fpread mifery and defpair throughout the whole extent of its dreary dominion.   But may *Britons* for ever keep out the horrid monfter; and maintain unblemifhed, from age to age, that happy conftitution, fo juftly admired and envied by the nations round them.

XXI. *The feveral fpecies of coins made of the fame metal, fhould be all of the fame finenefs.*

42. There are fome well meaning perfons, who allow all the preceding arguments againft debafing the ftandard, their full force; and yet propofe the coining of fmall fpecies of money of a bafer alloy than the prefent ftandard, but having in them the fame quantity of fine filver that the law now directs.   This expedient, they think, would be a means of preferving thofe coins from wear, and from being melted or exported.

As to the wear, it is not clear that this fcheme would anfwer the end: For, as the bulk and weight of the pieces would be both increafed, their wear muft alfo proportionably increafe; befides, this compofition would be more liable to wear than

I 3   purer

purer metal, as it would be more brittle
and lefs tenacious. But this confideration
is too minute, in comparifon of the many
inconveniences, that might attend any deviation from the common ftandard. As
to the increafe of bulk, I do not fee any
conveniency worthy of fuch an alteration,
that could arife from thence. There was
a time, when the largeft piece of coin in this
country, was no bigger than our prefent filver three-pence; and they had filver farthings, or the quarters of thefe: And were
our three-penny pieces now current, I do
not apprehend there would be any complaints of their want of bulk.

There may be a better and a neater
fcheme than this is, for preferving coins
from the melting-pot; but I do not chufe
to enter into that confideration at prefent.
There is an inconvenience in having too
great a variety of coins; and without manifeft neceffity, no alterations fhould be made
in the courfe of the mint, left any fufpicions of fome unfair dealings fhould be raifed
amongft the people.

The bafe coins here fpoke of, would probably be the laft that would be exported; as
the filver in them, by being commixed with
fo much copper, would really be leffened

in

in its value; and the public would not only
fuſtain this loſs, but it would alſo loſe the
whole value of the additional copper. But
in the preſent caſe, either the people would
refuſe taking theſe new coins at the mint
rates, and make diſtinctions between them
and other coins, as hath been before obſerved; or, if they paſſed current, a door
would be immediately opened for falſe coining. For, when the ſtandard of fineneſs is
much baſer than ours is at preſent, different degrees of deviations from it, are not
conſpicuous to the eye; and the preciſe
fineneſs cannot be ſo well aſcertained, even
by ſkilful aſſay-maſters. By this ſcheme of
coining baſe money, beſides furniſhing opportunities to counterfeiters amongſt our-
ſelves; we ſhould lay a temptation in the
way of foreigners, to commit the ſame
frauds.

Mr. RICE VAUGHAN in his diſcourſe *
of *coin and coinage* chap. VI. hath ſo well
handled this ſubject of baſe money, that I
cannot help making the following extract
from this ingenious author. He ſays, the
pretences for making baſe coins, were theſe
following, p. 45.

I 4   " *Firſt*,

* This was publiſhed in the year 1675, and contains many
uſeful obſervations relative to this ſubject.

" *First*, that there was no intention
" thereby to raife the price or diminifh the
" weight of *filver*, but that this money
" fhould be as good in intrinfical. value, as
" in the money of purer filver, fave only a
" fmall charge laid upon it for the coinage :
" then that by coining fmall pieces of a pen-
" ny, two-pence, or three-pence, or there-
" abouts ; the pieces, by the mixtion fhould
" have a greater bulk, and fo be preferved
" from lofs, which muft needs frequently
" happen by reafon of the fmallnefs of the
" pieces, if they were made of pure filver,
" fo likewife they fhould be preferved from
" wearing : and again, that the goldfmith
" fhould by this means be kept from melt-
" ing them, and the ftranger from export-
" ing them, becaufe the charge of refining
" them and drawing the pure filver out
" of them, would far exceed the profit.

" Thefe are the pretences by which bafe
" money was firft introduced, but if they
" be weighed againft the inconveniences,
" which have followed upon it, it will be
" found one of the moft mifchievous in-
" ventions that ever was found in mat-
" ters of money. I could hardly refolve
" with myfelf to infert this chapter in this
" difcourfe, becaufe having mine aim only
" at

" at the good of this ſtate, it ſeemed un-
" neceſſary to treat of this ſubject, ſince we
" have no baſe money in England; but
" when I conſider, that in ſome unhappy
" ſeaſon heretofore we have had baſe mo-
" ney; and that it is not impoſſible but that
" the like projects may again be received, I
" determined not only to treat, but to go
" through with it all at once, and not in-
" terrupt this diſcourſe any more with that
" ſubject.——The firſt inconvenience then
" of the great mixture of metals, is the
" falſifying of them; for both in reaſon it
" is too true, that by this mixture both the
" colour, ſound, weight, and the other
" more hidden qualities of the different
" metals, are ſo confounded as the falſity
" cannot be diſcovered, but with extream
" difficulty: and by experience it is veri-
" fied, that in all thoſe countries where
" baſe money hath courſe, the greateſt part
" of it is not coined by the ſtate, but either
" counterfeited by the natives, or brought
" in by ſeveral ſtrangers.
" *Secondly*, it is true that the *baſe money*
" was firſt coined in *France* of an intrin-
" ſical value almoſt equal to that of purer
" metals; and ſo it continues to this day,
" for ſo much of it as is coined by ordi-
" nance

" nance of the ftate, (the greateft part be-
" ing falfified:) But in moft other countries
" (as namely in Spain) the ftate itfelf, to
" raife a tribute on the people, hath ex-
" treamly falfified the intrinfical value ; by
" which means both the ftate hath for gain,
" coins much more than there is occafion
" to ufe, and there is incomparably much
" more counterfeited by others, fò as the
" mifchief doth hourly multiply.

" *Thirdly*, the values of money are con-
" tinually raifed from time to time, which
" is no new device (as is already more par-
" ticularly declared) the *bafe money* muft
" then in proportion be likewife raifed,
" which cannot be done by increafing the
" value of the particular pieces ; for, being
" of fo fmall price, the fractions would be
" irreconcilable ; fo as there is no other
" way left to raife the bafe money, but by
" coining new, of a weaker intrinfical va-
" lue. I would then gladly know what
" becomes of all the old *bafe money* ; either
" it is melted down by the *Bullioners*, which
" is the name in French of thofe, who by
" culling and trying of coins, make their
" profit to melt them ; or it is tranfported
" by ftrangers, fo as in effect the ufe of *bafe*
" *money* doth bring that inconvenience,
                                    " the

" the avoiding whereof was made one of
" the chiefeſt pretences for coinage of it.

" *Fourthly*, it is truly obſerved, that in
" all thoſe countries where *baſe money* is
" current, there the price of gold and ſil-
" ver is daily raiſed by the people, not only
" without the ordinance of the ſtate, but
" contrary to, and in deſpight of all prohi-
" bitions to the contrary, which draws with
" it extream diſorders and miſchiefs; ſo it
" is in the *Low Countries*, ſo it is in *France*,
" ſo in *Germany*, and in *Spain*; although
" the ordinance for the value of the gold and
" ſilver, may ſecurely be maintained by this
" help, that no foreign coin is there current;
" yet when you come to change black mo-
" ney for ſilver or gold, you ſhall there find
" how the people raiſe the price to you
" of the purer money. But in *England*
" and *Muſcovia*, where no *baſe money* is in
" uſe, there the people never raiſe the price
" of gold and ſilver (except by ordinance
" of the ſtate it be directed,) neither doth
" experience only try this concluſion, but
" reaſon alſo; for the people, when they
" ſee the money of baſe and uncertain mix-
" ture, do diſeſteem it, and in compariſon
" thereof do eſteem the money of purer gold
" and ſilver above the proportion, and ſo do

2   " raiſe

" raiſe the price of it ; and this eſteem is
" not meerly out of opinion, for that really,
" that piece of baſe money which hath as
" much fine ſilver as a penny, is notwith-
" ſtanding not worth a penny, becauſe the
" mixture makes that you can't extract this
" penny in pure metal without loſs and
" charge : And if the people do hold this
" baſe eſteem of this mixture, which hath
" in it the intrinſical value for which it is
" current ; how much more baſe eſteem
" muſt they hold of that mixture, which
" they know hath not near in it that intrin-
" ſical value, for which it is current, and
" how much more muſt they needs raiſe
" the ſilver ? And certainly *baſe money*,
" when either it is at firſt coined much in
" the intrinſical value, under the extrinſi-
" cal, or is by degrees brought unto it,
" and long ſo continued, doth in the end
" breed either *inſurrections* among the peo-
" ple, or rejections of it ; whereof the ex-
" amples of *inſurrections* are very frequent,
" and therefore I will forbear to inſtance in
" them.   But cannot omit one example of
" *rejection*, becauſe it is ſo freſh in memory,
" which was in *Ireland*, in the end of the
" reign of Queen *Elizabeth* ; which coun-
" try although it was newly vindicated from
                                          " rebel-

" rebellion, and did patiently endure all the
" imperious directions which a late fresh
" victory did bring with it; yet as soon as the
" exchanges of base moneys sent thither did
" cease in England, it was instantly rejected
" there, and would not pass current for so
" much as in the true intrinsical value it was
" worth, but was bought up at under-rates
" by such as made profit by melting it.

 " *Fifthly*, the dishonour that accompa-
" nies base money is of a more important
" inconvenience than all the rest; for what
" can be more dishonourable than to have
" the image of the prince, or the mark of
" the public attestation impressed upon false
" and counterfeited stuff? And if there be
" gain made of it, it is a manifest breach of
" the publick faith.—As for the remedies
" of this inconvenience of *base money*, I do
" leave those countries to struggle with them
" that are afflicted with it; for us in Eng-
" land the remedy is plain and easy, which
" is mainly and constantly to keep it out."

I have now gone through all the arguments, or rather pretences, that I have met
with, for debasing the standard of money.
The combating of so many vulgar errors
and prejudices, as I had to encounter with,

was

4

was to me a tafk fufficiently irkfome and
difagreeable; but if my honeft endeavours
towards removing thofe pernicious miftakes,
fhould be attended with fuccefs, I fhall think
my labour well beftowed.   The fubject certainly deferves the niceft difcuffion; and in
the handling of it, I have been the more
particular, as it feems to be a matter of no
fmall moment, that people in general fhould
underftand the true nature of money : This
would keep them upon their guard againft
any bad projects that might be offered ;
and difpofe them readily to receive any
fuch regulations about coins, as would be
for the public and their own benefit ; for in
truth, and it were to be wifhed more people underftood it, thefe two interefts are
infeparable.

POST-

P O S T S C R I P T.

Of STANDARD MEASURES.

THE utility and neceffity of having ftandard meafures, are very evident; and at the firft eftablifhing of thefe, it is quite indifferent what are the fpecific quantities affumed: The firft round pebble, and the firft ftrait ftick that came to hand, would make as good ftandard meafures, the one of a pound, and the other of a yard, fuppofe, as any that could be fixed upon. But I do not know whether it hath been duly attended to, that all ftandard meafures, whether of weight or extenfion, muft, in the nature of things, be *units*; that is, a ftandard properly fo called, muft be one determinate individual thing. The parts and multiples of this ftandard, wherever made by art, can only be confidered as approximations to the truth, or to thofe parts and multiples, which they are fuppofed to reprefent; and thefe will be more or lefs accurate, according to the fkill and care of the artifts employed in making them. Thofe artificial parts and multiples of the true ftandard, when made with due care, might be kept in proper

places

places as ftandards, for the comparing of others with them. But the true original ftandard, to which thefe *artificial* parts and multiples are referred, muft be, as above obferved, one individual thing, not fubject to doubts and fcruples, arifing from human in-accuracies in the forming of it. Upon this principle, there can be in the exchecquer but one ftandard weight; fuppofe this to be the *Troy-pound*; then the ounces, and their mul-tiples there to be met with, are to be deem-ed only as artificial approximations to the juft weights, intended by them refpectively; and this may be deemed fufficient for all common purpofes. A law then fhould declare explicitly, what piece, or pieces taken conjunctly, of metal now in the ex-checquer, is the real ftandard weight of the kingdom. * No more than this is neceffary to make the ftandard unit we have been fpeaking of; and if we have no fuch thing, it is a reproach to this enlightened age.

It is a pity that we have two forts of weights, *Troy* and *Avoirdupois*; but one of thefe

---

* The ftandard fhould be one clean piece of metal, kept un-der the locks of fome of the principal officers of ftate; and, I think, it fhould not be acceffible to any one, without their per-fonal prefence, if not of a certain number of other privy-counfellors. All the ufe that there need be made of this ftand-ard, would be for the adjufting of duplicates or reprefenta-tives of it, which might be kept in the feveral offices, as thofe

thefe being made the ftandard, and I think for many reafons that that fhould be the *pound troy*; it may be fufficient, after comparing the weights we have of each together, to declare in parts not lefs than grains, what proportion a pound of the one bears to the other made the ftandard. The law, by only naming the different parts of each, and declaring the proportions which they feverally bear to the whole, will fettle their quantities exactly, without leaving or creating thofe doubts that the inaccuracies of human art are liable to.

In like manner, if a *yard* be our ftandard of extenfion; this fhould be a clean ftrait metalline rod, with its ends fmooth and of a proper figure; or that extenfion laid betwixt two points upon a rod of a greater length. This rod being for conveniency divided as accurately as can be into parts; the feet and inches there expreffed, are to be deemed neverthelefs only as artificial approximations to the true ftandard. The longitudinal ftandard, as here the yard,

K

muft

thofe things called ftandards are at prefent. Thefe, being adjufted with due care and exactnefs, together with their artificial parts and multiples, the law might declare to be fufficiently exact, or near to the true ftandard, for common ufe. And to thefe all perfons might have recourfe at fuch proper feafons as the law fhould direct, upon paying of very moderate fees.

muſt be the real and only ſtandard of all
other meaſures, whether ſuperficial or ſolid.
Suppoſe a *gallon* is our ſtandard meaſure of
capacity ; if we would avoid difficulties and
abſurdities, the way of making this ſtandard is, by declaring how many cubic inches
make a gallon, and not by appointing a certain veſſel to be that meaſure ; but it might
be declared with propriety enough, that
ſuch a veſſel is ſufficiently near to the true
gallon. It would be a greater abſurdity
ſtill to ſay, that ſuch a veſſel, as a buſhel
for inſtance, ſhall contain or meaſure ſo
much, and alſo weigh ſo much of any thing.
For weights, and meaſures of extenſion, are
utterly incomparable. But it would be no
abſurdity to call a certain weight of corn,
for inſtance, by the name of buſhel, provided that at the ſame time all reference to
meaſure be excluded.

Theſe obſervations about ſtandard weights
and meaſures, may perhaps be deemed foreign to our ſubject, but they are of conſequence, and I could not expect a fitter opportunity of offering them to the public.

The End of the Second Part.

Printed in the United States
by Bookmasters

Printed in the United States
By Bookmasters